The Arctic Diary of
Russell Williams Porter

Eskimo girl

The Arctic Diary of

Russell Williams Porter

Edited by Herman Friis

University Press of Virginia

Charlottesville

THE UNIVERSITY PRESS OF VIRGINIA
copyright © 1976 by the Rector and Visitors
of the University of Virginia

First published 1976

End papers are reduced reproductions of printed maps compiled by Russell W. Porter. See chap. 9, n. 32.

Library of Congress Cataloging in Publication Data

Porter, Russell Williams, 1871–1949.
  The Arctic diary of Russell Williams Porter.

  1. Arctic regions. 2. Porter, Russell Williams, 1871–1949.
I. Title.   G606.P67   919.8 [B]   75–45375
ISBN 0–8139–0649–0

Printed in the United States of America

Something hidden. Go and find it. Go and look behind
the Ranges—
Rudyard Kipling, "The Explorer"

Eskimo

Foreword

RUSSELL WILLIAMS PORTER was born on December 13, 1871, in Springfield, Vermont, to Frederick and Caroline Porter. His father was an inventor and toy manufacturer who prospered during Porter's youth by producing and selling 75,000 baby carriages annually.

Porter entered the sophomore class at Norwich University in 1889 after attending Vermont Academy in Saxtons River for two years, and in the fall of 1890 transferred to the University of Vermont. The following year the family was faced with financial reverses, and Porter went to Boston to seek employment to pay for his education. It was there, in 1892, at the old Academy of Music, that Porter heard Robert E. Peary describe his reconnaissance across northern Greenland. Porter later said that he scarcely knew what struck him. "All I knew was that nothing would stop me 'til I had gone to the North." This was his "Arctic fever." He asked for a job on Peary's next expedition to the Arctic but was rejected after his elderly mother wrote Peary and begged him not to take her son. Porter would not be dissuaded, however, and in the summer of 1894 he made a voyage to Greenland with Frederick A. Cook on the ill-fated *Miranda*, as this book describes, returning in the fall to his architectural studies at the Massachusetts Institute of Technology.

As each spring rolled around, Porter, dreaming of the North and irked by confining indoor work, would become restless, and by the time the first polar ice was broken he was gone. Finally, in 1906, the North lost its lure, and, except for a canoe trip to Labrador in July 1912, he ignored its call. He settled in Port Clyde, Maine, and in 1907 married the postmistress, Alice Belle Marshall.

In the Arctic, primarily because of his work as an astronomer, there was born in Porter a fascination for the stars, which led to his subsequent career in astrophysics and optics. While living in Port Clyde, he made his first reflecting telescope in 1910 with a two-inch mirror. Later, he and Albert Ingalls, a member of the Board of Editors of *Scientific American*, established the hobby of telescope making. It became apparent to Porter that the fascination he experienced in looking at the stars with a telescope he made with his own hands was equal to his appreciation of the mechanical perfection needed to combine the laws of optics and mathematics in creating the instrument. To Porter this new challenge seemed comparable to that of the Arctic.

Porter moved to Boston in 1915 and taught architecture at the Massachusetts

Institute of Technology for two years. Then, in 1918, he went to Washington, D.C., to contribute to the war effort by working in optics at the National Bureau of Standards. He returned to his native Springfield in 1919 at the behest of his old friend James Hartness (later governor of Vermont), who owned the Jones and Lamson Machine Company. There, he worked out designs of precision tools involving optical elements, one of which was a garden telescope, an instrument beautifully ornamented with scrolls and leaves and having a six-inch $f4$ mirror. Fewer than one hundred were made and sold at $400 each. Today they are collectors' items.

Porter had been in Springfield only a short time when he brought together a group of machinists from local industries and taught them to make telescopes. In 1923 he organized the Telescope Makers of Springfield. Their clubhouse, Stellafane, built on a hilltop outside of town, attracted amateur astronomers from miles around and eventually from many states to compare notes and models.

In 1928, when George Ellery Hale acquired the funds from the Carnegie Institute to build a 200-inch telescope, he invited Porter to join the project in Pasadena and to assist in its design. The Porters settled near the California Institute of Technology, where the telescope was to be designed and finished before its final housing on Mount Palomar, a prominent 6,140-foot peak in the Coast Range mountains about forty-five miles north-northeast of San Diego. Porter remained at Cal Tech for two decades. His knowledge of astronomy and his artistry in preparing drawings smoothed the way for, and provided close control of, the instrument's development.

With the advent of World War II, the building of the 200-inch telescope was temporarily abandoned. Porter remained busy, though, preparing much the same kind of excellent mechanical drawings for government defense projects.

Porter began his Arctic diary about two years after settling in California. He wrote it from earlier diaries, sketchbooks, color notes, photo albums, on-the-scene pastels—anything of a descriptive nature that he had. His remarkable memory served him nearly as well as his mementos. That work has resulted in the present volume.

Porter died on February 22, 1949, at age 77 in Pasadena and was buried in Port Clyde. Through the intercession of his friend Albert Ingalls and others, the moon crater Clavius B was named Russell W. Porter by the International Astronomical Union in August 1970.

I wish to express my appreciation to Berton C. Willard, the author of a forthcoming biography of my father, for his help; to *Scientific American* for allowing me to quote from the April 1949 issue; to Ruth P. Doyle of the Editorial Branch of the National Archives, who has carefully reviewed the manuscript and made significant editorial contributions; to David Eggenberger, Director of the Publications Division of the National Archives, who has contributed his talents to, and is responsible for, the preparation of the manuscript for publication and for valuable suggestions in the development of the format; and to Virginia Stradford of the Center for Polar Archives, who typed and assisted in proofreading the manuscript.

CAROLINE PORTER KIER

Whale Sound woman—the eye squint is characteristic.

Preface

RUSSELL W. PORTER wrote his Arctic diary in 1930–31, at age 60, while living in Pasadena, California. He moved to Pasadena in 1928 to work as a key scientist on the design and construction of the 200-inch telescope—a remarkable undertaking—that was completed on Mount Palomar and dedicated in 1948.

During the period 1894 through 1912 Porter accompanied ten arctic expeditions, on which he served as artist, surveyor and cartographer, scientist, and astronomer. Generally, he kept rather careful, legible diary and journal notes and records of scientific observations. Significantly, he took many photographs and, as an accomplished artist, made numerous pencil sketches, watercolor and oil paintings, pastel sketches, and pen-and-ink drawings; these represent some of the most valuable graphic records of the Arctic for this period of pioneering geographical exploration.

The Russell Williams Porter Family Collection, Record Group 401 (27B), was presented to the National Archives for deposit in the Center for Polar Archives on February 28, 1974. Subsequently, several smaller accretions were made to the collection. Caroline Porter Kier, Porter's daughter, was the donor of all the papers from Portland and Port Clyde, Maine, which are included in the National Archives Gift Collection of Materials Relating to Polar Regions, Record Group 401. Among these papers are the three items that make up the manuscript of the Arctic diary: (1) Porter's long-hand pencil text of pages 22–92 of his initial version of the manuscript (pp. 1–21 were not received); (2) his ninety-four page typescript of text, written during 1930 and the early part of 1931, which is the basis for this publication, and a three-page list of ninety illustrations to be incorporated in the text; and (3) the ninety pencil sketches, apparently made by Porter from his numerous pieces of artwork, memory, and the rough pencil sketches in his diaries and journals.

Porter's daughter typed the typescript from her father's long-hand manuscript during the summer of 1931. The typescript has been copy edited for publication, a process that included not only correction of spelling and punctuation but some stylistic revision. Geographic names in the text have been reviewed for agreement with the decisioned or approved names in gazetteers compiled and published by the

United States Board on Geographic Names. Decisioned or approved names appear in parentheses. There are a few geographic names, probably of local origin and without official recognition, for which no verification can be obtained.

An attempt has been made to document as fully as possible the subject matter in the text in order to acquaint the reader with sources of related information and with historical materials in the National Archives Center for Polar Archives and in other depositories. This documentation also includes reference to related published materials that are useful in corroborating and amplifying specific subject matter. Legends for the artwork are Porter's.

On November 25, 1968, the National Archives accepted from the Honorable Ralph Flanders, senator from Vermont, seventy-nine nitrate film negatives said to have been taken by Porter in the summer of 1899 during the Peary arctic expedition in the *Diana*, which was commanded by Herbert L. Bridgman, president of the Peary Arctic Club. These negatives have been converted to positive prints.

The National Archives also received from Berton C. Willard, in April 1975, a thirty-four minute tape recording of his narration entitled "The Art and Life of Russell W. Porter" and 134 35mm color slides. These have been accessioned as Gift of Historical Materials From Berton C. Willard, Record Group 401 (89).

HERMAN R. FRIIS
Director, Center for
Polar Archives

The Arctic Diary of
Russell Williams Porter

The arctic goddess

Introduction

ARCTIC FEVER. The term is manifestly a paradox. For how could anyone run a temperature sitting on a cake of ice within ten degrees of the North Pole? Tropical fevers, yes. Tropics and fevers go hand in hand as anybody knows, but to get all "het up" over the North is a contradiction.

However, there are plenty of fellows, perhaps to their sorrow, who well know the insidious disease, who enter the great white spaces year after year, only to return to civilization beaten and discouraged. Sometimes they go once too often and don't come back. And if you cornered them for a candid expression of their feelings in the matter, I am sure you would receive first an embarrassing silence and then a vague answer—none of them alike.

Some might say, "Why sure, I know what it is. It's wanting to know what's around the corner—'beyond the ranges'—just plain curiosity after the unknown." Others would ring in a variation, "Well, the Pole of this old ball of ours is endowed with properties all its own. There's nothing like it anywhere. Think of the kick of standing on that spot around which so many theories have been woven. It's unique." Then there are those who would say that the search for the North Pole was just a big athletic stunt; hundreds had tried for the prize and failed, and these very failures intrigued them.

But somehow these interpretations of arctic fever do not seem to satisfy me. The call, in my own case, came suddenly, kept on calling for twelve years, and then as suddenly ceased. Let us liken it to an invisible personality, beckoning even as a siren of old to lure one on, over the icy portals and into her embrace. My arctic goddess has given me many thrills, many heartbreaks, many crushing defeats, few favors. At each crestfallen retreat I could almost hear her saying, "Go. This domain of mine is not yet ready for human eyes to look upon. Not for millenniums will I let you in to stay. Go, and be thankful you're alive." Yet always after a month or so of civilization came that magnetic pull that brooked of no resistance, could not be denied.

How well I remember those words of Peary's in the old Music Hall in Boston in 1892 on his return from the first crossing of northern Greenland, telling his audience of the topsy-turvy conditions surrounding a person standing at the North Pole.[1] Out of a clear sky that evening came to me the indefinable lure known as

[1] This was one of a series of lectures by Robert E. Peary to obtain funds for his second north Greenland expedition, 1893–95. Although adversely affected by the silver panic, Peary, with support from Maj. James B. Pond, head of the Pond Lecture Bureau, was able to raise enough

arctic fever, which took the best of twenty years of my life before I had had enough. Day and night I could see nothing but the pictures Peary threw upon the screen, snow-driven figures toiling over the endless wastes of Greenland's ice cap, drawn towards the point where all longitudes meet, where there is only one direction—south—and where there is no time: where one step towards the sun gives you noonday, and one step away from it midnight.[2]

I was twenty-one and a student at the time this bug hit me, working my way through the Massachusetts Institute of Technology.[3] Nothing more unfortunate could have happened to a young man just starting out in life with his chosen profession, which in my case was architecture. As I look back now on the situation through a perspective of forty years, it seems incredible that I could so willingly have thrown over whatever business prospects and advancement might offer for the years of toil, and exposure, and hardships that were bound to come to anyone trying to locate the North Pole. All those interested in my welfare immediately threw cold water on it. It raised dire forebodings in the minds of my parents as I persistently brought the subject into the conversation.[4] But I cannot remember ever once arguing with myself against such obvious folly. It seemed as clear as day: I must "look beyond the ranges" and see for myself. It is doubtful that a bribe of any kind could have overcome the temptation. The arctic goddess was beckoning.

---

money to subsidize this expedition. See Pond, *Eccentricities of Genius: Memories of Famous Men and Women of the Platform and Stage* (New York, 1900). For a list of Peary's lectures, his itinerary, and his correspondence with Pond, see the Adm. Robert E. Peary Papers, ca. 1865–1945, National Archives Gift Collection of Materials Relating to Polar Regions, Record Group 401 (1), hereafter cited as the Peary Papers.

Publications by Peary concerning this expedition include *Northward over the "Great Ice": A Narrative of Life and Work along the Shores and upon the Interior Ice-Cap of Northern Greenland in the Years 1886 and 1891–1897*, 2 vols. (New York, 1898); "A Reconnaissance of the Greenland Inland Ice," *American Geographical Society Journal (Bulletin)*, 19 (1887), 261–89; "A Proposed Exploration of Greenland," ibid., 23 (1891), 157–93; "The Party and Outfit for the Greenland Journey," ibid., pp. 256–65; "The North Greenland Expedition of 1891–92," ibid., 24 (1892), 536–58; "Journeys in North Greenland," *Geographical Journal* (London), 11 (1898), 213–40. See also Josephine (Diebitsch) Peary, *My Arctic Journal: A Year among the Ice-Fields and Eskimos* (New York, 1893).

[2] These slides probably were made from negatives of photographs taken during Peary's 1891–92 expedition. See the Peary Papers for this collection.

[3] Here Porter began to study architectural design in 1893.

[4] For correspondence between Porter's parents and Peary, see the Peary Papers.

AFTER THAT EVENING in the old Music Hall, nothing would do but to try to contact Peary and beg him to take me on as a member of the party he was then organizing for his second expedition. To give the reader an idea of how badly I had become inoculated with the virus of this arctic fever, I saved enough from my small earnings to journey to Washington to put my case before the commander in person.[1]

The result was negative and a great disappointment. "All right," he said, "you have given me your qualifications. There are a great many applications already filed, and I will let you know my decision later by letter."[2] And I returned to Boston.

I remember the wait for that letter seemed interminable. When it finally arrived, the contents were to the effect that with the great number of men from whom he must choose I must not consider it any reflection on myself that he was unable to accept me.[3] It was some years later that Dean Burton of M.I.T., a classmate of Peary's at Bowdoin College, told me the following: "Do you know, Porter, that Peary was on the point of signing you up for his 1893 trip when he received a letter from your mother imploring him not to take her son to the Arctic; that she would come to Washington on her hands and knees, if necessary, to intercede for her son. Well, Peary did the only right thing."[4]

[1] In a letter of May 16, 1893, Peary acknowledged Porter's correspondence of May 11 and 14 (presumably written at Bingham House in Philadelphia). On May 31, Mrs. Caroline S. Porter wrote Peary from her home in Vermont, "My son Russell W. Porter has been home a few days and gave me the startling information that he has been in correspondence with you." Therefore, if Porter did go to Washington to meet with Peary, his visit occurred probably after May 14 and before June 4, the period during which Peary was at his Twelfth Street residence.

[2] There is no evidence of this quotation in either the Peary Papers, RG 401 (1), or the Russell W. Porter Papers, 1890–1940, National Archives Gift Collection of Materials Relating to Polar Regions, Record Group 401 (27–B), hereafter cited as the Porter Papers. Peary, however, in his letter of May 16, 1893, did indicate to Porter that he hoped circumstances would permit them to meet on the train between Philadelphia and Trenton.

[3] There is no correspondence from Peary to Porter on this subject among the Peary Papers or the Porter Papers.

[4] See correspondence between Peary and Mrs. Caroline S. Porter among the Peary Papers. Alfred Edgar Burton was a close friend of Peary's during their undergraduate days at Bowdoin College in Brunswick, Me. He graduated from Bowdoin in 1878 with a degree in civil engineering.

So that was that. Not long after, I ran across a paragraph in the paper stating that Dr. Frederick A. Cook was organizing a popular excursion to the arctic regions and would shortly appear at the Mechanics Building in Boston with some Eskimos and arctic paraphernalia. You may be sure that I was right there when the doctor arrived. I found him a very affable young man, as badly bitten with the fever as myself. He had been through one winter as surgeon with Peary and was now advertising a trip in a chartered vessel for a summer's cruise up the west Greenland coast—something new to arctic exploration. Cost, $500.[5]

I must have talked the doctor blue in the face about the price, for he finally said, "Well, Porter, I'll take you on for $300 and make you the artist and surveyor to the party, and in that way you can help work your passage. We plan to leave New York about the first of July." And thus was launched my first voyage beyond the Arctic Circle.

The Eskimos he was exhibiting had been left stranded by some promoter at the World's Fair in Chicago, and the doctor, out of the goodness of his heart, was taking care of them and seeing that they were returned to their home in Labrador.[6]

It will be unnecessary to go at length into the vicissitudes of this trip, the first attempt of its kind to make the Arctic a popular place for summer excursions. It was persistently followed by ill luck and ended disastrously in shipwreck. To anyone who desires the harrowing details, I refer him to the official narrative entitled *The Last Cruise of the* Miranda, by the historian of the party, Henry Collins Walsh.[7] It

---

From 1879 to 1882 he was a draftsman and topographer with the U.S. Coast and Geodetic Survey. In 1902 he became dean of the Massachusetts Institute of Technology after having taught topographical engineering there for twenty years.

[5] Dr. Cook was surgeon and ethnologist on Peary's first north Greenland expedition, which left New York on June 6, 1891, in the barkentine *Kite*, a sealer commanded by Capt. Richard Pike. For ethnological notes and correspondence, see the Peary Papers. See also chap. 10, pp. 156–62.

[6] The World's Columbian Exposition held in Chicago in 1893.

[7] *The Last Cruise of the* Miranda: *A Record of Arctic Adventure*, ed. H. C. Walsh (New York, 1896). Dr. Cook's contribution to this publication was "The Greenlanders," pp. 172–79.

WHALE SOUND

SOUTHERN GREENLAND

BAFFIN LAND

Three styles in dresses

certainly put a black eye on the Arctic as a popular summer resort, for it has never been tried since.[8] It was said at the time that, had our ship been a wooden whaler instead of an iron vessel, there would have been a different story.

Some fifty-odd men from all walks of life—professors, sportsmen, and merchants, old and young—comprised the personnel.[9] Most of them had never experienced hardships. As the *Miranda* started to back out of her pier on the East River, the wires to the engine room in some way became crossed and she forged ahead, smashing into the head of the dock as though bound across the city. "What the hell you think you're doing?" some wag yelled from ashore. "Think you're taking a short cut to Greenland?"[10]

All went well until one morning in the fog off the Strait of Belle Isle while we were seated at breakfast. We heard a commotion on deck, followed by a severe shock to the whole ship, and the dishes went sliding to the floor. When we reached the deck, there was a huge iceberg towering above us. Blocks of ice lay on the forward deck.[11] Slowly, the vessel pulled away, and an examination showed her stern badly crushed and the hawse pipe broken.

So back we went to Saint John's, Newfoundland, and into drydock for repairs. Here several passengers elected to go home, others not so badly scared preferred transferring to a local steamer for a summer in Labrador, while the rest of us stayed by the ship and were soon pounding down a meridian headed for Greenland.

The sight of our first pan ice near Cape Farewell (Kap Farvel) was never to be forgotten. I have seen a great deal of it in the twenty years that have followed. Our captain probably knew that an iron ship was about as much good as pasteboard if she struck any of it, for he turned tail and tried to reach the coast by circling into the

---

[8] This was true, perhaps, when Porter wrote this account. Now, however, Icelandic Airlines, for example, flies between Reykjavik, Iceland, and southeastern Greenland, and there are summer tours to Spitzbergen, Greenland, and the North American Arctic.

[9] Porter's Journal, 1894, pp. 2–3, among the Porter Papers, describes the passengers and crew of the *Miranda* and gives a detailed account of the voyage. This handwritten account is illustrated with photographs and pencil sketches.

[10] According to Porter's Journal, 1894, pp. 1–2, these remarks were made by a man on board the lighter about to collide with the *Miranda*.

[11] For reference to this accident, see ibid., pp. 22–26.

She struck the berg above the waterline, smashing in the star-board hawse pipe. Several tons of ice lay on the deck.

9

west. Our landfall proved to be near the little town of Sukkertoppen, populated by a few hundred half-breed Eskimos under Danish colonization. We stayed only a short time, a sort of courtesy call as it were, and then started to go up the coast.

The climax to the summer's cruise came right there. The Greenland coast is poorly charted. At the entrance to this harbor was a submerged reef (uncharted), and right over this reef the good ship *Miranda* essayed to go. We could feel rather than hear the ship's bottom being torn out of her as she went over and into deep water.[12] There was a mad dash to swing out the lifeboats while the carpenter sounded the hold for water. When he reported a dry ship, the panicky feeling subsided. But I was for the first time thoroughly scared and tasted what I think Stewart White calls "copper." I have tasted this a few times since—at times of great fear when events, the outcome of which seemed fatal to me, were transpiring: once during a subsequent shipwreck in Franz Josef Land and once when I was having a scrimmage with a polar bear and my gun was useless. It is a quite definite taste, akin to the sensation one gets when placing certain electrodes upon the tongue that will generate a slight current.[13]

"Chips," the carpenter, also reported to the captain that the ballast tank was full of water and the hole evidently was below the ballast tank. On limping back into the harbor we had so recently left, the result of a council of war decreed that some of the party should go up the coast in search of succor—it was reported that American schooners were wont to fish somewhere off the coast for halibut—and that one of these vessels should be found and induced to accompany us home. For it was agreed by all to be unsafe to try it alone.

I was overjoyed to be selected by Dr. Cook to be one of the rescue party.[14] The governor of the village donated the services of a couple of Eskimos as guides, and we were soon sailing along the rocky coast, crossing the mouths of huge fjords that ran for great distances into the interior. As we were crossing these fjords, we had

[12] The *Miranda* left Sukkertoppen at 6:30 A.M., the crew was in excellent spirits, and Porter had just finished breakfast when the accident occurred (ibid., p. 58).

[13] See chap. 8, pp. 104–6, and chap. 7, p. 90.

[14] "Our crew is composed of the following men: Dr. Cook, Mr. Rogers, Mr. Ladd, Mr. Thompson, myself, and four esquimaux, nine in all and we shall take a small schooner belonging to the Governor [Mr. Baumann] which he has put at our disposal" (Porter's Journal, 1894, p. 60).

Iceberg

glimpses of the white upturned shield of the great inland ice cap. There was no night, only dusk, for we were nearing the Arctic Circle. We crossed it the next day and were at last in the arctic regions. I doubt if the others experienced the thrill of passing this imaginary line at N 66⅔° dividing the temperate from the frigid zones of our earth, but I had scanned that dotted line on maps too often not to be enthused. During the eighteen crossings since, I have seen Neptune come over the side of the ship to shave the novices with great ceremony, but they never had the kick that accompanied this first transit.

It did seem that our luck changed for the better as the Circle was crossed. At the first town, Holsteinsborg, we were told that a Gloucester schooner was somewhere off the coast and that the governor had dispatched a kayaker to intercept it and bring it in.[15] The sight of those old salts in their oilskins and sou'westers, swinging up the path from the shore, was good for our souls. Skipper Dickson, captain of the three-masted schooner *Rigel*, six months out from Gloucester, heard our story without comment and asked for time to confer with his crew, who were on shares. His name is now a household word in many homes in the States, where they bless him for his decision to abandon his cruise and come to our relief.[16]

Such was their verdict. We all went aboard and in a little over a day were back at the side of the stricken *Miranda*. Calling in the passengers who were investigating the fjords and islands of the vicinity, Captain Dickson took a quantity of fishing gear and salt out of the hold and threw them overboard; by squeezing in like sardines in a can, we could be accommodated. A cable was passed over the stern of the *Miranda* to the bow of the *Rigel*, the steamer taking the schooner in tow, and the return to civilization was begun. The plan was to bring off provisions from time to time.

I can remember trying to persuade Dr. Cook before leaving Sukkertoppen to let me remain in Greenland for the winter and return to Copenhagen next fall on a Danish ship.[17] Professor Dyche of the University of Kansas also was of the same

[15] Ibid., pp. 69–70.
Kayaker is an Eskimo word for a person in a kayak, a fully decked-in skin canoe propelled by a double-bladed paddle.
[16] "Capt. Geo. W. Dixon Schr Rigel, No. 41 Commonwealth Avenue Gloucester Mass." is written at the top of an unnumbered page in Porter's Journal, 1894.
[17] See ibid., pp. 43–45, 48, 52, and 60. In Sukkertoppen, Porter wrote his mother a letter on Aug. 10, 1894: "I have been busy photographing the distant mountains capped with snow and the shimmering snow fields beyond" (Porter Papers).

We crossed the Arctic Circle without much difficulty. Or rather,
as a child I dreamed we would find it much like this.

mind, but for some reason it fell through, probably because no permission had been obtained through the Department of State and the Danish government.[18]

There still remains a striking recollection of the dancing Eskimos. With the aid of two fiddlers they circled round and round over the oily floor of an old warehouse. The scuff-scuff of their sealskin boots, the half-wild music of the violins, midnight revelry in broad daylight—all this framed an unforgettable picture.[19]

On leaving Greenland our luck was not to last long. The second day out we ran into rough seas, and the ship signaled that she was making bad weather, that the ballast tanks were beginning to give way under pressure they were not intended to stand, and for us to stand by and be ready to take on board the ship's crew.[20]

The summer was getting on. We were working south, and the nights were increasing. Around midnight a red light on the *Miranda*'s stern announced the ship's abandonment. Soon the crew arrived in lifeboats and came tumbling aboard. I distinctly remember one of the second engineers as he fell in over the gunwale, spilling a lot of silver knives and spoons from his pockets onto the schooner's deck. Liquor also was strong on the breath of several of the crew.

When they were all aboard, the mate of the *Rigel* went forward and with an ax severed the hawser that held us to the doomed ship. The last we saw of her was the red light as she slowly moved away in the darkness. There was one live pig left aboard, and all our personal possessions, including some twenty Eskimo skin boats, or kayaks, traded for at Sukkertoppen. I have since been told that this loss of their boats proved a calamity to the little settlement, as it took away their only means of securing a livelihood, and accounts in a measure for the strict rules laid down by the Danish authorities when it comes to permitting foreigners to visit Greenland.

The rest of that "popular excursion to Greenland" can be told in a few words: over one hundred men on a sailing vessel only a hundred feet long. As food ran low we subsisted on salt halibut fins. My bed in the afterhold was literally on fish and salt. There was just room to crawl along on the salt without bumping one's head on the deck beams. The memory of that fish smell is very vivid. For the younger men it

[18] Louis Lindsay Dyche. See *Who Was Who in America*, vol. 1.

[19] Porter's Journal, 1894, contains two pages of music in his handwriting. One, the score, is entitled "Esquimaux Song"; the other, apparently the Esquimaux lyrics, "Somandshilsen." The music is allegro in $2/4$ time.

[20] For an interesting account of the *Rigel* towing the *Miranda* and the crisis that occurred, see ibid., pp. 70–79.

She slowly disappeared in the darkness, her sole passenger a live pig.

wasn't so bad, but some of the older passengers, particularly Professor Brewer of Yale and Prof. G. Frederick Wright of Oberlin, suffered keenly.[21]

There was beginning to be an alarming shortage of water by the time we made the Labrador coast, but here we obtained more, and fresh fish also. After riding out a gale in the Gulf of Saint Lawrence, we sailed into Sydney harbor, Cape Breton Island, with all hands accounted for. Here the party broke up, some going on by train and the majority taking a ship to New York via Halifax.

But even here, on another ship, bad luck seemed to follow us. Entering Long Island Sound, near Cuttyhunk, about breakfast time (all our accidents seemed to happen at that time), and going along full speed in a dense fog, the ship cut a coal-laden schooner in two. We saw the crew being drawn down by the suction of the wreckage as they were frantically trying to launch their only boat. Only one, the mate, was picked up. After cruising about for an hour, the ship went on again into the fog.[22]

It was that evening, the end of the trip, that the Arctic Club was formed. In the smoking room we proposed to perpetuate the friendships made under such strenuous circumstances: to meet once a year, and over a bounteous board, surrounded by every comfort, we would live over again the popular excursion to Greenland. The Arctic Club was later merged with the Explorer's Club of New York.[23]

The sequel is scarcely more encouraging than the trip itself. It seems that the insurance companies refused to pay Captain Dickson and his crew anything for abandoning their fishing cruise and bringing us home. Had the *Miranda* succeeded in getting back, our rescuers would have been paid heavy salvage. As it was, they got nothing. So we took it upon ourselves, as a sort of moral obligation, to see that they were reimbursed. All proceeds from the sale of the book narrative and personal contributions have been enough, I understand, to almost cancel this obligation.

[21] William H. Brewer and George Frederick Wright were geologists and members of the scientific group on the *Miranda*. For their biographies, see *Who Was Who in America*, vol. 1. See also Brewer, "Atmospheric Dust in the Arctic Regions," in *Last Cruise of the* Miranda, pp. 148–61; and Wright, "Glacial Observations in Labrador and Southern Greenland," ibid., pp. 162–71, and *Greenland Icefields and Life in the North Atlantic, with a New Discussion of the Causes of the Ice Age* (London, 1896).

[22] Porter's Journal, 1894, pp. 98–102, gives a detailed account of this accident, in which the *Portia* collided with and sank a fishing schooner, resulting in the loss of five of the six men aboard the schooner.

[23] Among the Porter Papers is a pencil sketch by Porter of the proposed insignia or letterhead of the Arctic Club.

One hundred men on a vessel less than a hundred feet long

Jensen and his whalebone. This man is over six feet tall.

Chapter 2 1896

IF THE READER has followed me thus far in my first flirtation with that icy goddess residing beyond the Arctic Circle, who had treated me so shabbily, returning me to civilization with only the clothes on my back (and those untanned sealskins), he would justly conclude that I had found what was coming to me, that I had learned my lesson, and that I had decided that the North was not all I had imagined it to be. Well, the reaction was quite the opposite. Those fugitive glimpses of the shimmering ice cap far back in the interior of that continental island, that week with the natives when the door to the North was barely opened before it was closed, the haunting melodies of the dancing Eskimos accompanied by scuffing feet over a sand floor, the nights without darkness—all served only to raise the fever to a higher pitch and a stronger determination to go farther and to see more.

My employer greeted me cheerfully. "Ah, monsieur l'explorateur! Have you had a pleasant summer? Would you like to get down to work again?" In this way Professor Despradelle of M.I.T. welcomed me into his office each time I returned.[1] He evidently knew it was hopeless to try to dissuade me from this folly, but he was always ready to take the prodigal back and set him to work. As I leaned over the drawing board, I could hear the ice pans grinding together, the raucous cries of the gulls, and the guttural ejaculations of the Eskimos.

The following summer must have been an off year with arctic expeditions, for it found me in Boston with my nose to the grindstone, earning the wherewithal to put me through Tech. I lived in Watertown and walked to Boston to the institute each morning with a classmate, Alfred Shaw, who lived in one of the Newtons and who had much of my own love for adventure and the wanderlust.[2] When we were not canoeing and camping weekends up the Charles River, we planned all sorts of

---

[1] Porter borrowed money to study architecture at the Massachusetts Institute of Technology, where he was a special student from 1894 to 1898, working with Constant Désiré Despradelle, Rotch professor of architectural design.

[2] Alfred V. Shaw, class of 1896, Massachusetts Institute of Technology, lived in one of the subdivisions of Newton, Mass., about six miles from the center of Boston.

expeditions to out-of-the-way places. We even discovered that Boston was on an island and circumnavigated it. The trip, which finally took shape, was a walking tour through England. We found that one could work his passage over on a cattle boat, have a month or so over there, and return on the empty boat with nothing to do. We visited the stockyards in Watertown, looked up the foreman who was to be our boss on the ship, and, as it were, booked our passage then and there. However, some fellow who had already tried it warned us that, if the foreman was so disposed, he could make it mighty uncomfortable for us, and he advised us to pick a good one.

As matters turned out, the warning proved quite unnecessary. One day Professor Burton (already alluded to in the previous chapter)[3] told me that Peary was going north that summer and had asked him to organize a party of scientists to accompany the expedition and be landed at some convenient place for scientific work.[4] Would I care to go along? If so, he would try to find some way to pay my passage on the grounds that I already had some arctic experience. Would I go along? *Would I*?

So Shaw and I didn't take the cattle boat that year, nor any other year, but we did go north together the following year on a whaler.

That summer was by far the pleasantest I had ever experienced in the North. My duties were those of commissariat, in charge of the food and camping equipment for our party's stay in big Umanak Fjord half way up the west coast.[5] There were the geologist Barton, the government geodesist Putnam, who was to swing the pendulum for gravity determinations, the sportsman Dodge, and myself.[6]

Going by rail to Sydney, we found the whaler *Hope* awaiting us. Mrs. Peary, her

---

[3] See chap. 1, n. 4.

[4] For information about the working relationship between Burton, who was in charge of the scientific expedition to Umanak, north Greenland (1896), and Porter, see correspondence between Porter and Peary, especially for May 24 and 28 and June 3 and 26, 1896, in the Peary Papers, RG 401 (1).

[5] The first principal fjord north of Disko Island on the west coast of Greenland.

[6] George Hunt Barton and George Rockwell Putnam were members of Peary's expedition to Greenland, 1896. See Barton, "Evidence of the Former Extension of Glacial Action on the West Coast of Greenland and in Labrador and Baffin Land," *American Geologist*, 18 (1896), 379–84; and "Glacial Observations in the Umanak District, Greenland [Scientific work of the Boston party on the sixth Peary expedition to Greenland. Report B.]," *Technology Quarterly*, 10 (1897), 213–44; and

Eskimo boy, Umanak—Only one native of this town was thought to be pure Eskimo. The settlement had some three hundred inhabitants in 1896.

daughter Marie Ahnighito, and Albert Operti, the arctic artist, were aboard.[7] For our skipper we had Sam Bartlett of the now-famous family of ice navigators. Taken altogether, it was an ideal personnel.

Throughout the summer the arctic goddess smiled upon us. With stops in Labrador and the Hudson Strait to swing the pendulum and the customary courtesy call at Disko, we passed up the Wigat (Vaigat).[8] Our party landed at Umanak while the *Hope* went on farther into the North after the big meteorite.[9]

The little settlement of Umanak was presided over by Governor Knudsen, a Copenhagen University man, who with his wife seemed overjoyed to see people from the outside world. While the Danish government scowled at any attempt at foreign penetration, these poor isolated people could not do enough for us. They had been here for years. Their only contact with the outer world was one ship a year. In fact, at the next and last town north, Upernavik, the governor had a one-year-old newspaper placed at his plate each morning. Perhaps this was just as well, so long as he could only talk to an Eskimo.

I was given a little house of my own, where I set up my studio and painted full-size

<hr/>

Putnam, "The Greenland Expedition of 1896 under Charge of Professor A. E. Burton," *Proceedings of the Davenport Academy of Natural Sciences*, (1897) 359–62; "Results of Magnetic Observations on the Greenland Expedition of 1896," *Terrestrial Magnetism and Atmospheric Electricity*, 2 (1897), 32–34; and "Magnetic and Pendulum Investigations [Scientific work of the Boston party on the sixth Peary expedition to Greenland. Report A.]," *Technology Quarterly*, 10 (1897), 56–132.

According to Peary's Journal "The Voyage of the *Hope,* 1896," p. 198a, the Peary Papers, Dodge was Arthur M. Dodge, photographer from Hampton Falls, N.H. See also Porter's Journal, 1896, p. 10, in the Porter Papers. RG 401 (27–B).

[7] This reference is to Peary's wife, Josephine Diebitsch Peary, and daughter, who was born at Anniversary Lodge, Bowdoin Bay, northwestern Greenland, Sept. 12, 1893; to the artist Operti, who traveled to the Arctic with Peary in 1896 and again in 1897 (see chap. 3, p. 36) as special correspondent for the *New York Herald*, was the first to make casts of north Greenland Eskimos, and painted and sketched the Arctic and polar explorers; and to Sam Bartlett, who was one of the leading ship captains with extensive arctic experience (see chap. 5, p. 57).

[8] A fjord that marks the north coast of Disko Island.

[9] See Peary, "The Cape York Ironstone," *American Geographical Society Journal (Bulletin)*, 26 (1894), 447–88; and *Northward over the "Great Ice,"* vol. 2, "Summer Voyages of 1896–1897."

Matelina

watercolor portraits of the natives. Even this far north it was difficult to find purebloods. The women posed in their best skins, with colored ribbons tied tight about an upstanding topknot, the particular color worn denoting her social standing in the community. If it was red, you could take it for granted she was unmarried and eligible. If it was blue, she was married. And if it was black, it denoted widowhood. Sometimes we found a little white mixed in with the black and on inquiry found that these ladies who had lost their husbands were still in the market for others. The badge of disgrace was green—neither maid, nor wife, nor widow.

They were all short, plump and oleaginous, but a few were not without charm. Little Matelina Sigurdsen appeared one day at the studio with an arctic bluebell peeking out from her red ribbon. But by far the most difficult subject was a mother with her infant, which she carried in her hood on her back. The baby was very restless and was continuously sucking on a strip of white blubber.

The rest of the party were off somewhere making a reconnaissance, and I was having the time of my life. Knocking off at noon, there was dinner at the governor's and billiards for one öre a cue. "You must play for something, if only an öre," he said. One öre is about a quarter of a cent. Then I went over to the house of the Lutheran priest. While the governor talked fluent English, the minister could not speak a word of it, nor I a word of Danish. So we got out a lexicon and taught each other a few phrases in the other's tongue. Danish is said to be the easiest of all foreign languages for the English-speaking people to learn. As a slight return for his kindness I tuned his piano, which was sadly in need of tuning.

Before our party started up the fjord to measure the movement of the enormous glacier there, I made a watercolor of the governor's house and presented it to Mrs. Knudsen. Six years later, returning from Franz Josef Land, I stopped at Copenhagen and went up to Jutland to call on Mr. and Mrs. Knudsen, who were then retired and living on a farm.[10] He took me into their bedroom and, pointing to the wall,

[10] Porter was returning from the Baldwin-Ziegler expedition, 1901–2. See chap. 7, p. 96.

24

Half-breed Eskimo

said, "Do you recognize that?" There was the watercolor of their old home in faraway Greenland.

All being ready for the glacier and inland ice, we started up the fjord in two boats heavily loaded with supplies, camp gear, Eskimos, dogs, and sleds. The fjord was full of enormous icebergs majestically moving slowly out to sea on their long voyage to dissolution in the warm waters of the Gulf Stream. The Eskimos were in a joyous mood, the accompanying kayakers going through all sorts of maneuvers. Perched high on a berg ahead of us was a lone gull. A native handed me my gun and pointed to the bird. I knew it was a hopeless shot, but I accommodated the fellow and was more surprised than the others to see the bird fall. I had evidently made an impression on the Eskimos as a mighty hunter and, in order to maintain my prestige, refused to fire another shot. The governor later told me I was known as "heap big shot."[11]

The Greak Karajak (Great Qarajag) Glacier—one of the largest in the world—was busy with her summer litter of icebergs.[12] "Calving" is the expression used, and very likely has its origin in the groaning sounds always heard when the glacier is about to be delivered of several million tons of ice. The fjord was literally choked with the monsters.

Making our camp at a hut built by the scientist Drygalski,[13] we set up stakes in a line on the glacier's surface, and then followed several miles up the shore of this ice stream. We started out over its treacherous surface, heading towards the interior of the big island. The going was rough and slippery, for it was almost clear ice, the

[11] See Porter's Journal, 1896, p. 49.
[12] For a description of the glacier, see ibid., pp. 51–55.
[13] Erich von Drygalski, in 1892–93.

We found the fjord choked with enormous bergs.

ascent being quite marked. By the time camp was made, we had lost the land entirely and had nothing but a white unbroken expanse clear to the horizon.[14]

Recently, there has been considerable activity among scientists in exploring the characteristics of this great mass of ice covering the greater part of Greenland. It has now been crossed, crisscrossed, and lived on, and its depth found to be several thousand feet thick.

One more day in this inhospitable place was quite enough, and we dropped down to land and the everlasting mosquito. On the way our course was crossed by a real river of ice water flowing rapidly between steep walls of pure blue- and green-tinted ice.

This trip gave me my first camp on ice, the first of many hundreds to come.

At the hut we measured how far the stakes had moved down stream, and then backtracked for Umanak. On the way Williams and I took an Eskimo, crossed the fjord to the Nugsuak Peninsula, and had a try for caribou. Although we saw several, they were too far off. Perhaps we were very poor shots. Anyway, we returned empty handed. While on this hunt, I saw my first hanging glacier. There were several of them, advancing down through the ramparts that held back the great ice sheet like a dam. In fact, it looked as though the titanic dam had given way and, like viscous syrups, they were pouring through, each one the color of robin's-egg blue.[15]

At dinner one day with our kind host, the governor, a man's name came into the conversation casually, resulting in an interesting outcome. The name was Bradford. He was an artist of repute who must have had a bit of the arctic fever, for he found a patron to fit out a ship for him to go north and paint.

The *Panther* brought him ultimately to Umanak in 1869, where Governor Knudsen was already established. He remembered the artist well.[16] I told Governor Knudsen that I had called on Mr. Bradford's wife in New Bedford the previous

---

[14] See Porter's Journal, 1896, pp. 53–55.

[15] See ibid., pp. 68–78.

[16] For an account of William Bradford's visit to Greenland in his steam yacht, the *Panther*, in 1869, see Isaac I. Hayes, *The Land of Desolation: Being a Personal Narrative of Observation and Adventure in Greenland* (New York, 1872). See also Bradford, *The Arctic Regions, Illustrated with Photographs Taken on an Art Expedition to Greenland* [1869] (London, 1873).

Like an egg in its nest, the glacier hung over the lake.

year, and she had said that one of her husband's last desires was for a rock from the land he loved so well for a headstone to his grave.

"We'll get one," said the governor. "We'll get one right away. I'll have the Eskimos go up the fjord now and bring it in." And so he did. When Peary returned from the North, he (Peary) had the boulder taken aboard. At Sydney he had it placed on a freight car billed through to the States. Later I journeyed to Fair Haven (Fairhaven, Mass.), across the bay from New Bedford (Conn.), and found the grave and the granite boulder with a polished face bearing an inscription.[17]

Bradford's paintings of the North have never been excelled. A great many were reproduced as chromos. He took with him a photographer who made many beautiful photographs of glaciers and icebergs by the wet-plate process which had recently come into use. They appeared in an edition de luxe and found their way into the homes of many of the royalty in England.

I have but one more incident to describe which took place towards the end of this 1896 trip.[18] We had crossed Baffin Bay homeward bound and put into Cumberland Sound so that Putnam might swing his pendulum for the last time. I usually assisted him in this work. They rowed us ashore and landed our tent and instruments. A substantial pier of brick was built, the transit mounted thereon, and the tent erected. The night being clear, the necessary observations were made on the stars. We then turned into our sleeping bags (one on each side of the pier) and went to sleep.

Sometime during the night I was awakened by Putnam, who was shouting, "Oh, oh, oh, Porter." The transit, a heavy instrument of brass and cast iron, lay on the ground, badly broken.

[17] Among the Peary Papers is the following telegram, dated Oct. 13, 1896, from Porter: "Forward bowlder Mrs. William Bradford Fair Haven, Mass. Bill to me." Also included is a letter, dated Oct. 20, 1896, from Porter, stating that Miss Mary E. Bradford, a daughter of Mrs. William Bradford, sent heartfelt thanks to Peary for getting and sending the granite boulder that was placed on Bradford's grave.

[18] See Porter's Journal, 1896, pp. 101–3.

"Oh, oh, oh, Porter."

Putnam (now head of the U.S. Lighthouse Service) was a very quiet fellow, always bearing an unruffled exterior.

"Porter, just what were you thinking of?"

"I—I must have been dreaming, Mr. Putnam. Yes, I was dreaming."

"What about?"

"A bear. I thought he was coming into the tent, and I grabbed at him."

"Oh, yes, that explains everything." And pointing to the smashed transit he remarked dryly, "There is your bear. You certainly got him."

Well, in one way it was not so serious. The last observation of the season had been taken a few hours before. Some thirty-five years later I reminded Putnam of the incident. He had not forgotten it.

Chapter 3 1897

ON THE WAY HOME from the North on the expedition just described, and while stopping in Cumberland Sound for Putnam to swing his pendulum, I passed a fascinating afternoon with a Scotchman who was running a whaling station at Niantilik (Niante Harbour), an island on the south side of the sound.[1] He told me of unexplored reaches of the hinterland, Baffin Land (Baffin Island), which is larger than New England and the Middle Atlantic states, of lakes reported by the natives to be so great that they could not see the opposite shores, and of possible tribes living there and unknown to white people. He also reported a tragedy of the winter before, of a young Dane living at another whaling station down the coast, who had badly frozen his feet and was in urgent need of surgical aid.

This news prompted Peary to stop in at the station, which was called Cape Haven, at the entrance to Frobisher Sound (Frobisher Bay). The call resulted in our taking young Jensen aboard and bringing him to Boston for treatment.[2] Another passenger, a retiring missionary, picked up at the Scotch station also filled me with intriguing accounts of the little-known interior, and before the voyage was terminated my plans for the following year were already forming in my mind.[3] I would try to find someone to finance a modest expedition of my own and, with perhaps one companion, attempt the penetration and clearing up of this region, at that time a blank on the charts.

I had just received a scholarship at the institute (M.I.T.) and put in the winter on postgraduate work at Tech, working mornings in an office with Professor Despradelle.[4] Every available moment of spare time was spent searching for the

---

[1] "Black lead is now a Scotch Station but only purchased recently from the Americans. There are two buildings in which the man in charge, Capt. Sheridan, the pastor, Mr. Pick and the doctor live" (Porter's Journal, 1897, p. 109, Porter Papers, RG 401 [27–B]).

[2] See Porter's Journal, 1897, pp. 111–14.

[3] "Mr. Pick, the missionary with us . . . is returning to his home in southern England" (ibid., pp. 111–12).

[4] See chap. 2, n. 1.

wealthy patron who was to grubstake the budding explorer. At one time the funds were almost in my hands. Dr. Franz Boas of Columbia (and now president of the American Association for the Advancement of Science), who had spent a winter with the Eskimo in Baffin Land and to whom I appealed for help, interested the *New York World* in a plan to have me collect arctic material to be donated to the American Museum of Natural History.[5] Just why the project fell through I cannot now remember, but I do distinctly remember my feeling of despondency on my return to Boston, with only the consolation of Dr. Boas' parting words, which were, "Remember, Porter, you may count on me for anything I can do. Your plan is a good one and ought to be realized. If you do put it over, I'll provide you with the necessary scientific instruments."

The break came with a letter from Peary. "I'm going north again this year to make another try for the meteorite. Why don't you organize a party of students for the summer in Frobisher Bay. I will land you at Cape Haven on the way up and pick up the party on my return in the fall, and you can remain there for the winter."[6]

It was my only chance. I rather doubted my ability to organize the party, but there was no harm trying. It was the spring of the year, and I advertised in the college papers to provide passage to and from Baffin Land and all necessary equipment

[5] Boas was a specialist in the anthropology of the Arctic. See *Dictionary of American Biography*, Supplement Three, 1941–45 (1973), pp. 81–86; Walter R. Goldschmidt, "The Anthropology of Franz Boas: Essays on the Centennial of His Birth," *American Anthropological Association*, Memoir No. 89 (Menasha, Wis., 1959), pp. 1–165; and Robert H. Lowie, "Biographical Memoir of Franz Boas, 1858–1942," *National Academy of Sciences, Biographical Memoirs*, No. 24 (Washington, D. C., 1947), pp. 303–22. For examples of Boas's arctic work, see his *The Central Eskimo* (Lincoln, Neb., 1964); and "Baffin-land. Geographische ergebnisse einer in den jahren 1883 und 1884 ausgeführten forschungsreise," *Petermanns Mitteilungen Ergänzungsheft*, No. 80 (Gotha, 1885), pp. 1–100. A large collection of Boas's papers are filed in the archives of the American Philosophical Society in Philadelphia.

For information concerning funds and backing for Porter's expedition to the Arctic, see correspondence in the archives of the American Museum of Natural History in New York City and the following letters from Porter, 1897, among the Peary Papers, RG 401 (1): March (Boston), to Judge Charles P. Daly; and Mar. 21 (Watertown, Mass.), Mar. 30 (Boston), Apr. 19, May 16, 20, 25, and 30, and June 2 and 16 (Watertown), to Peary.

[6] For Porter's comments regarding the expedition he planned for the summer of 1897, see his letter to Peary, Jan. 10, 1897, from Watertown, Mass., in the Peary Papers.

Eskimo men, women, children, babies, and dogs

and transportation for two months' hunting and fishing in Frobisher Bay. We would leave about July 1 and be back in time for college in the fall.[7]

Well, it worked. In no time at all a half dozen young fellows were found, glad to pay me $500 apiece for the privilege.[8] On paying Peary for his (Peary's) share, which I think was $300, there was enough left to outfit the summer party and my own work the following spring. The only thing left was to find a way to get home myself the following year. It is not generally known that, aside from a stray whaler or two, there is no possible access to the arctic regions without a ship of your own. I finally arranged with the owner of the Scotch station already referred to, to give me passage on his vessel to Dundee, Scotland.

With everything set I approached my old camp mate Shaw.

"How about a year, old man, with the Eskimos, astraddle the Arctic Circle? Want to go?"

Of course, there was only one answer. He was as badly bitten with arctic fever as I.[9]

It was an auspicious departure as the *Hope* pulled out from Tea Wharf in Boston. Mrs. Peary and daughter, and I think Operti, the artist, were aboard.[10] My crowd of students were congenial to a man. Jensen, much recovered from his winter in a hospital, was returning to his station. A bridal couple, Hugh Lee and wife, were to spend their honeymoon in the far North.[11] The voyage "down the Labrador" was

---

[7] A resumé of this expedition is included in Peary, *Northward over the "Great Ice,"* 2: 552–618.

[8] Among the Peary Papers are (1) a brochure entitled "Peary's Arctic Expedition, 1897," that contains the statement that "the expenses of transportation to and from whatever locality may be selected for the summer's work will be $450 per individual, or $2,500 for a party of six," and (2) Porter's correspondence for January to June 1897 about the solicitation of funds, especially from the American Geographical Society of New York, and the Smithsonian Institution and the National Geographic Society of Washington, D.C.

[9] In addition to Porter and Alfred V. Shaw (see chap. 2, p. 19), the party included Delano Fitzgerald of Baltimore, a physician; his son Charles Galt, of Harvard University (class of 1900); Frederick Grosvenor Goodridge of New York and Harvard (class of 1896); J. Neilson Carpender (or Carpenter) of New Jersey and Harvard (class of 1896); and A. Hollis White of Braintree, Mass.

[10] See chap. 2, pp. 20–22.

[11] Hugh J. Lee was a much-respected member of Peary's arctic expeditions of 1893–97. With his bride, the former Florence Augur Leonard of Meriden, Mass., he accompanied Peary on the 1897

Eskimo women washing dishes

uneventful. We put into a harbor or two for fresh fish or to allow Captain Sam to visit some one of his several relations distributed along the coast. Finally, the *Hope* landed us at Cape Haven and proceeded on her way north.[12]

Frobisher Bay—or Sound—has a history that makes it quite unique in a way, for it records the first gold rush in the Arctic. Martin Frobisher induced Queen Elizabeth to fit him out with several vessels as a result of his story of finding gold on a previous voyage. It is recorded in the proceedings of the Hakluyt Society that about fifteen ships loaded down with colonists and gold seekers left England in 1576. Some of them never were heard from. Some did make the passage and wintered in the Bay, and of these only a few returned, but without gold.[13]

It was this record that induced Captain Hall (who afterwards met his death in an attempt to reach the Pole) to spend a winter in the bay trying to locate the gold seekers' settlement and to retrieve what relics remained.[14] He found scarcely a trace

---

expedition to Greenland to obtain the large ahnighito meteorite for the American Museum of Natural History in New York City. Lee and his bride spent much of their honeymoon at Godhavn in western Greenland and returned to New York with Peary in the *Hope*. See Lee's diaries and correspondence among the Hugh Johnson Lee Papers, National Archives Gift Collection of Materials Relating to Polar Regions, Record Group 401 (59). See also his "Peary's Transections of North Greenland, 1892–1895," *Proceedings of the American Philosophical Society*, 82 (Philadelphia, 1940), 921–34.

[12] The landing of Porter's party is recorded in the "Log of the Baffin Land Expedition of 1897 Kept by Charles Galt Fitzgerald," p. 18, the Fitzgerald Papers, National Archives Gift Collection of Materials Relating to Polar Regions, Record Group 401 (63).

The skipper of the *Hope* was Capt. John Bartlett (see chap. 5, n. 3).

[13] George Best, *The Three Voyages of Martin Frobisher, in Search of a Passage to Cathaia and India by the North-west, A.D. 1576–8*, reprinted from the 1st ed. of *Hakluyt's Voyages*, with selections from manuscript documents in the British Museum and State Paper Office by Richard Collinson (New York, 1963); and Sharat K. Roy, "The History and Petrography of Frobisher's 'gold ore,'" *Field Museum of Natural History*, Publication No. 384 (Chicago, 1937), pp. 21–30.

[14] Charles Francis Hall, *Life with the Esquimaux: A Narrative of Arctic Experience in Search of Survivors of Sir John Franklin's Expedition* (London, 1865); Chauncey C. Loomis, *Weird and Tragic Shores: The Story of Charles Francis Hall, Explorer* (New York, 1971); C. H. Davis (ed.), *Narrative of the North Polar Expedition, U.S. Ship* Polaris, *Captain Charles Francis Hall, Commanding* (Washington, D. C., 1876); and J. E. Nourse (ed.), *Narrative of the Second Arctic Expedition Made by Charles Francis Hall . . . During the Years 1864–69* (Washington, D.C., 1879).

Salmon falls at the head of Frobisher Bay

of the old adventurers. You may be sure I had this fascinating possibility in mind as a side issue to my own work.

We must have presented a strange appearance as our fleet of two whale boats, loaded to the gunwales, debouched into the bay for the summer's cruise. Persuaded to go along with us for the princely pay of one plug of tobacco a week each, three or four Eskimo men were bringing their entire families and worldly belongings. Men, women, children, babies, a lot of dogs and puppies. How they were ever stowed away in the boats in addition to our own crowd is a miracle.

At the first camp-out, after rowing about twenty miles, it was discovered that a box containing all our knives, forks, and spoons was missing. What to do? Go back after them and waste two valuable days out of our precious time? Never! They were murderous-looking substitutes we carved out of wood from the packing cases, but they served. I think the fellows would have been willing to eat with their fingers rather than go back. Of course, with the Eskimos it didn't matter. Food reaches their digestive organs with no such aids to eating.

The summer's outing in the bay came well up to the expectations of the party. A detailed account of the trip will be found in one of the bulletins of the American Geographical Society for the year 1898.[15] Much of the region was unexplored, and the novelty of not knowing just what would show up around the next corner kept every man on the qui vive. We soon picked up enough Eskimo words to get along.

The bay was found to be some hundred miles to its head, thickly strewn with islands, and among these islands were heavy tidal currents that might have made a lot of trouble had the natives not been with us with their uncanny knowledge of winds, weather, and tides. There is a rise and fall of forty feet at the head of the bay, comparable to that in the Bay of Fundy.[16] As a consequence, when we made camp at low tide, the boats had to be dragged considerable distances over the rocks to the selected campsites. Whale boats are heavy affairs to move, but they were handled quite easily by laying down runways of oil-barrel staves, over which they could be slid to higher levels.

It was not long before I overheard a word from one of the Eskimos that sounded

[15] See Porter, "Frobisher Bay Revisited," *American Geographical Society Journal (Bulletin)*, 30 (1898), 97–110. There is a map at the end of the article showing Porter's route.

[16] "The tides in the bay vary from twenty to thirty feet, and when setting in opposite directions, as they sometimes do among the islands, create currents which are remarkably erratic and powerful" (ibid., p. 98).

_S.S._ Hope _in an ice pack_

familiar. It was "Kodlunarn." This meant "white man's island."[17] I asked the fellow where it was, for it undoubtedly was the site old Frobisher had picked out for his colony of gold seekers over three hundred years before. He pointed to the place, and that night we camped somewhere near the historic spot. Shaw and I roamed around over the rocks, looking for evidence of former white man's occupancy, but not a thing rewarded our search. Hall, some forty years previously, had found what he took to be a trench where a boat might have been built and a chunk of cast iron that might have been a cannon ball.[18] We (Shaw and I) left the place the next day, intending to return later in the year for a systematic search. As matters turned out, we never revisited the spot. Since then, I understand, McMillan has taken up the work, but I have no knowledge of his findings.[19]

At the extreme end of the bay we found a river tumbling over the rocks in a ten-foot fall—about the only stream of any size emptying into the bay. Here we were soon to lie in the lap of plenty, for the Eskimos began spearing huge salmon, and the first day out Shaw and I returned with a large buck reindeer (arctic caribou). Old Euawpig, our head Eskimo, told me it was only three "sleeps" to one of the big lakes in the interior where the stream had its source.[20]

Not far from the camp was a rounded hill, about two hundred feet high, literally packed with fossils and later found to indicate the Devonian horizon.[21] None of us were geologists. So we gathered only those specimens that caught the eye. I shall never forget the look on the face of the curator of the American Museum[22] when, the following winter, I dropped on his desk an old sock full of unprotected fossils,

[17] "The island is called 'Kodlunarn' by the Eskimos, or 'White Man's Island,' there being still a tradition among them of a number of ships coming from the east manned by white men" (ibid., p. 100).

[18] The cannon ball was discovered in the general area of Countess of Warwick Sound (Porter, "Frobisher Bay," p. 99).

[19] This may be Donald Baxter MacMillan. See his biography in *Who's Who in America*, vol. 36.

[20] For a detailed description of one of the lakes, see Porter, "Frobisher Bay," p. 102.

[21] "Silliman's Fossil Mount" of Hall, a limestone table-topped mountain (ibid., pp. 102–4).

[22] The American Museum of Natural History in New York City.

Tooloogah—The Raven (Baffin Land)

with the remark "What are they worth?" I believe they were later studied and described by Dr. Schuchert of the Smithsonian Institution as several new varieties, to the names of which were appended the designation "Porteri."[23]

That must have been a red-letter day for me, for, in addition to discovering fossils new to science, some of the fellows came into camp that night from a day's hike to the west with the announcement that they had found a lake some ten miles long. "And, by right of discovery, we have called it Lake Porter." This, by way of passing, is the only time my name has gotten on the maps. Of the many thousand square miles of unknown territory I have since surveyed and mapped, other names have been applied. It is not considered good form for an explorer to name anything for himself.

On our return down the west coast we ran across an old Eskimo campsite of several tent rings. Euawpig said they were very old and had been occupied by natives who came across the land from Hudson Strait.

Farther on we stopped in a beautiful small bay surrounded by towering cliffs, with a crystal-blue glacier coming down from a miniature ice cap. I named it Boas Glacier.[24]

The snowfield from which the Boas Glacier has its source is a remnant of the ice cap that once covered much of our continent and is the most southern ice field in North America. It is inconsiderable in size and probably diminishing. Shaw and I set out stakes on the glacier, lining them up with stone cairns on either shore, intending to revisit the place the following year to determine how fast the ice stream was moving.

It was at this camp that I acquired great distinction among the natives as "heap big doctor." Angekok, they call him, with supernatural powers of the medicine man. It

<hr>

[23] See Porter, "Frobisher Bay," pp. 103–4, for a footnote reference to a letter of Jan. 31, 1898, that Porter received from Dr. Charles Schuchert; Schuchert, "Notes on Arctic Paleozoic Fossils," *American Journal of Science*, ser. 4, 38 (1914), 467–77, for information about more conspicuous fossils from Frobisher Bay; and "On the Lower Silurian (Trenton) Fauna of Baffin Land," *U.S. National Museum Proceedings*, 22 (Washington, D.C., 1900), 143–77, for a discussion of fossils collected by the Porter party at Silliman's Fossil Mount in 1897.

[24] The glacier and its source are described in Porter, "Frobisher Bay," pp. 109–10.

The Boas Glacier

happened this way: On landing at the camp just described, we found quantities of ground blueberries growing. The Eskimos evidently craved fruit of some kind along with their diet of seal meat. Consequently, they gorged themselves with the berries, and the wife of Euawpig (the chief) came down with severe pains that probably were nothing more or less than just plain cramps. Euawpig, greatly excited, dragged me into his tent, where I saw his wife stretched out on the ground, moaning, her feet pressed against the bare stomach of another woman, who obviously was substituting for a hot-water bottle.

Well, I looked as professional as I could and felt her pulse, which seemed a little weak. Back in my tent I dug out an emergency kit, hitherto unopened, which Dr. Cook had kindly put together for my use in the North. Going over the labels on the various bottles, I came onto one "to stimulate the heart and kidneys." It was the only bottle referring to the heart. With this profound deduction, I returned to the sick woman and proceeded to dose the patient.

When ready to break camp the next morning, she was able to wobble down to the boat and Euawpig requested that I sit on the thwart beside her. By night she was fully recovered and my reputation established. For the rest of the cruise it was "Doctor this and Doctor that," and they came to me for all sorts of hurts, sprains, and pains. I am convinced those pills were far from what she needed—they might have killed her—but the psychological effect on the natives was incontestable.

On our return to the whaling station, we found the *Hope* already in from the North with the meteorite aboard. On shore at the station, Jensen took me into executive session.

"Porter, I am sorry to bring you bad news, but piblokto (dog disease) has taken off nearly all the sled dogs, and it will be quite useless for you to think of going into the interior next spring. You had better return to the States on the ship and try again some other time."

This, indeed, was a stunning blow. My first venture in the North to be thus knocked into a cocked hat. When would I get another chance? Shaw and I went into a huddle and talked it over. We agreed that it looked as though Jensen didn't want us to winter at the station, and unfortunately we were dependent on his good will for many things essential to our success. On several occasions the winter before,

Bringing home the bacon

Jensen had remarked, "Oh never mind this or that. I've got plenty of it," referring to different articles of food or equipment. I believe, had this climax come some years later, I would have seen it through and tried somehow to finish the job. Shaw was willing, but I decided (as I now look at it) to turn tail. And in all the years since, when I come across a bit of news that this man or that one had penetrated to the heart of Baffin Land and unlocked some one of its secrets, it has aroused a feeling of envy and resentment—resentment because I had come to believe it was my own preserve, and envious of the lucky fellow's chance.

On board, Peary said, "You and your companion are quite welcome to go home on the ship with us, but the ice pack outside is closing in on the shore, and you must have your things aboard by midnight. I have too much at stake"—and he pointed amidships, where the meteorite lay a captive in chains, and aft to his wife and daughter—"to take any chances of being caught here for the winter."

And so ended the Porter Expedition to Baffin Land—my first and last independent wooing of the goddess of the North—in failure.

Two adult Eskimo women alongside normal-sized white men

Chapter 4 1898

THIS CHAPTER will be a short one.[1] It describes a more or less erratic trip into northern British Columbia, to the headwaters of the Peace River. It really does not belong because I did not quite cross the Arctic Circle. It was a summer filled with the hardest kind of work and resulted in a seasoned conviction that gold *is* only where you find it and that the Indian cayuse is just one hell of an animal.

This was the year of the great Klondike rush. Gold, gold, gold! Tickets from Boston to Seattle, $25. Don't go to Alaska by water. Go overland with pack horses. Good gold prospects all the way, plenty of feed for the horses, plenty game, plenty everything. So read the advertisements.

And so picture three young greenhorns who had never seen a pack horse, deciding to go to the Klondike overland through British Columbia. Nothing to it.

Shaw had already gone on with one of my last year's party to a stake somewhere up the Alaskan coast. But he had a brother who sowed the seeds of unrest in my being until I finally gave in. The third victim, Ambrose Atwood, had never ventured scarcely beyond the Charles River.

Professor Despradelle showed no surprise when I announced my departure from the office.[2] "Eh bien, come back when you will. There is always interesting work to do here."

There was the long overland journey on the C.P.,[3] traveling tourist, where I had for a seatmate a prize fighter bent on starting a saloon in the silent North as soon as possible. And one dark morning I was dumped on the platform of Ashcroft Station, to see Atwood and Shaw huddled on a baggage truck.[4] They had preceded me,

---

[1] Porter's Journal, 1898, of this expedition is a pocket-size, leather-covered notebook containing sketches, sketch maps, and such information as names and addresses, grocery lists, and cooking recipes for field messes. Pages 20–61 cover the period May 3–Sept. 26, 1898. See the Porter Papers, RG 401 (27–B). A narrative account of the expedition, "Northern British Columbia. By pack train and dugout," apparently prepared by Porter for publication, is also among the Porter Papers.

[2] See chap. 3, p. 33.

[3] The Canadian Pacific Railway Company.

[4] Porter arrived on May 8, 1898, at 7 A.M. at Ashcroft Station in British Columbia, about fifty miles west of Kamloops.

purchased ten cayuses and camp equipment, and were camped three miles back in the hills "waiting for better feed along the trail."

"We have been advised by the wise not to be in too much of a hurry; to stay here for a month where the feed is good, get acquainted with our horses, and learn to throw the diamond hitch. We're camped back in the hills doing just that. Come on over to the main street and see the sights."

A typical western frontier town but fraught with feverish activity. Men astride wiry broncos, tearing up and down the street. Groups of swarthy faces on the corners in deep consultation. Presently, there is a commotion. Down the street comes a pack train headed north and manned by a party of eastern tenderfeet who have probably done nothing more strenuous than selling ribbons over a counter back home.

There's a shriek from a switching engine in the train yard, and something goes wrong with the bell mare. She objects and begins kicking. Soon she has her pack under her belly and proceeds to distribute the contents neatly over the dusty street. The kitchen horse follows suit. There go the pots and kettles. The rest of the train decide to stampede.

"We've seen this sort of thing every day or so," said Shaw, "ever since we arrived. I guess we better stay a little longer."

I guessed so, too, and was more than convinced later in the day when we arrived at camp and I was given a demonstration of how to put the stuff on the cayuse's back and how to make it stay there.

"These horses were sold to us for $25 apiece and guaranteed to have traveled together. The feed is none too good, so we haven't hobbled 'em. Just let 'em go where they choose."

They chose to go far—and in different directions as well. I found this out the next morning when we started out at sunup to find them. It was well along in the morning before we had them all in camp and could have our coffee. I might add that this goes also for the rest of the mornings for the summer, doing a day's work in getting ready for the day's run. Where feed was good, it was not so bad. But those morning hours! Hunting the little devils was no fun.

Major (Atwood's cognomen) said, after the horses were tied up to trees on the edge of the camp, "We are now picking out the best saddle horses for us to ride. I think this red one here is my oyster and I'm going to try him out."

He did and had just got his right leg over the saddle when the cayuse shot out from under him, and Major dropped to the ground like a plummet. He sat there as though glued to the earth, his head slowly turning from right to left, a look of hurt surprise suffusing his countenance.

My luck proved much the same as Major's, but Shaw did better. However, we soon decided we needed outside help. At the rate we were getting along, the Klondike seemed a long way off.

"There's two fellows camped up the creek about a mile. They're from Utah and look like the real stuff. Perhaps they'd help us."

We descended on their camp and recited our woes. One of them said, "Sure, I'll help you out. Show you all the tricks and go on a day or two with you to see you well started on the Telegraph Trail."[5]

Our benefactor proved a veritable godsend. Soon the diamond hitch became second instinct, and in a few days we hit the trail "a resounding whack," as Hamlin Garland says.[6] In fact, Garland followed us up over the same trail that summer. We felt quite like old-timers when the Utah cowboy left us.

Those days on the trip in were cut much on the same pattern. Up with the sun, rounding up the horses, breakfast of bacon and bannocks (fried pan bread), and the day's run of about fifteen miles, camp with wood, water, and feed available, and dinner of beans and more bannocks. Then to fill out the afternoon, we puttered about camp, mending equipment, treating the horses' backs for pack sores, writing up our diaries, and finally turning in. It was fly time, and we all wore netting over our faces, day and night.

Matters went fairly well for the first hundred miles or so, but after leaving Quesnel, where the famous Telegraph Trail really begins, our troubles began to accumulate. This much-advertised highway to the gold diggings was never intended for pack horses. It was laid out in the fifties when an attempt was made to communicate with Europe by telegraph via Alaska, the Bering Strait, and Siberia. Several hundred miles had been built through the wilderness when Cyrus Field laid the first Atlantic cable, and all work, of course, was then abandoned. Straight as the

---

[5] See Porter's Journal, 1898, p. 23.
[6] *Dictionary of American Biography*, Supplement Two, (1958), pp. 218–20.

Learning to pack

crow flies, this line was surveyed over mountains, down through swamps and muskegs, making the worst possible going for a horse.[7] Here and there remnants of the wire and insulators could be seen high up in the trees.

Gruesome evidence of tragedies of parties that preceded us became apparent. Dead horses mired beside the trail with their pack saddles on. At one campsite, cut into the bark of a tree was the terse remark "Stranded here two weeks. Lost the diamond hitch." At another camp we came across a party who had lost one of their numbers. They had been searching for him several days and were beginning to give up hope that he was still alive. They pictured him as going insane from the flies and mosquitoes. At the Blackwater a party of two men had lost their horses. We stopped here a week, helping them hunt. One day around noon the whole drove solemnly walked into camp.

At Stewart Lake I saw for the first time a Hudson Bay trading post, a rambling collection of log houses surrounded by a stockade. Here I received a setback. Before leaving the East, I had made arrangements with the American Museum to collect ethnological material from the Indians in order to bring back something useful for the summer's effort.[8] But a Catholic priest, Father Morice, had fore-stalled me, had combed the whole territory, and disposed of them to Lord Somerset a few years before.[9] Well, all right, there was still some unmapped country ahead of us which, if all went well, I could survey and clear up.

So on we went, and in another two hundred miles entered an old gold-mining region known as the Manson Creek diggings.[10] A lot of the yellow metal had been

[7] Information about this historical survey for a telegraph route is contained in William H. Dall, "Robert Kennicott," *Transactions of the Chicago Academy of Sciences*, vol. 1 (Chicago, 1868), pp. 133–226; Joseph Henry, "Explorations by Mr. Kennicott," *Annual Report . . . of the Smithsonian Institution . . . for 1863* (Washington, D.C., 1864), pp. 52–53, and "Explorations of the Hudson's Bay Territory, by Mr. Robert Kennicott," *Annual Report . . . of the Smithsonian Institution . . . for 1859* (Washington, D.C., 1860), p. 66; and James A. James, "The First Scientific Exploration of Russian America and the Purchase of Alaska," *Northwestern University Studies in the Social Sciences*, No. 4 (Chicago, 1942), pp. 1–276.

[8] The American Museum of Natural History in New York City.

[9] Porter wrote in his Journal, 1898, p. 57, that on Sept. 18 he called on Father Morice and had a long talk with him.

[10] A settlement on the Omineca River in north central British Columbia. For a description of the countryside and Porter's itinerary, see his letter, Aug. 17, 1898, to his mother among the Porter Papers.

Baldy—my saddle horse

taken from the creek beds here back in the seventies, and modern methods were now being introduced to tear down the benches with monitors. Here, Shaw found a letter telling him to meet his brother at tidewater. About this time a certain Captain Black appeared in camp, looking for a surveyor to run some water levels on his claims, begging me to help him.[11]

So the Shaw, Atwood, Porter gold-seeking expedition of 1898 busted up, all very friendly, and no hard feelings. We divided up our equipment, horses (what were left), food, etc., and bade each other au revoir. For a month or so I had a great time hobnobbing with the miners, watching them sluicing the gravel in the creek beds. It was fall now—warm days, frosty nights, no gnats to make life miserable.

Only a hundred miles farther north was virgin land to the cartographer (I was already on the arctic waterhead), but the summer was too far gone to reach it. My diary indicates that I had added gold fever to arctic fever, for it gives in great detail a plan for returning to Boston, organizing a company, and returning over the snow in the spring to develop several mining claims that looked promising enough.[12] I may say now that this attempt never got farther than an interview with some financiers who threw cold water on the whole proposition on the ground there was not enough money in it. They wanted at least 700 percent profit.

September found me taking the back trail—"screwing my nut," as the miners called it—with one cayuse and two Indians, walking. At the Hudson Bay post I exchanged the cayuse for passage down the Stewart and Nechako Rivers in the company's dugout going out for winter supplies.[13] At Quesnel I took the stagecoach down the Fraser Valley to Ashcroft and boarded the train for Boston.

No, the wily bronc and the inquisitive mosquito failed to draw me away from my former love. The arctic goddess was still beckoning. Within a year I was conniving with Peary to revisit Greenland.[14]

---

[11] There is no information that Porter consented to help Black.

[12] Porter's Journal, 1898, contains on p. 7 a description of a claim made in the name of the American Consolidated Hydraulic Mining Companies, on p. 78 a description of his association with a Capt. B, on pp. 79–80 the statement that Capt. B "advises my organizing the company as soon as possible," on pp. 148–49 the names and addresses of six mining companies, and on p. 149 "Capt. C. N. Black, Phoenix Place, Victoria, B.C."

[13] For details of this return trip, see ibid., pp. 58–61.

[14] Porter was corresponding with Herbert L. Bridgman, secretary of the Peary Arctic Club. Bridgman was in charge of the *Diana*, which was sent north to provision Peary during the summer of 1899.

Chapter 5   1899

THIS CHAPTER will be shorter than the last, for although I organized a modest trip to Baffin Land (Baffin Island) this year, I remained behind.[1] The condition of my father's health was so grave that I dared not accompany the party. He passed away that summer about the time the *Lilly of the North* went on the rocks in faraway Labrador.

The main purpose of the voyage was to carry supplies to the American Whaling Station at Frobisher Bay and bring back the bone and oil accumulated there by Jensen the Dane.[2] The owner of the station, a Boston merchant who knew nothing of the job in hand, came to me for assistance. So I chartered the *Lilly of the North*, mentioned above, a two-masted schooner from Saint John's, skippered by one of the famous Bartlett family, and met it at Halifax, where she took on her cargo.[3]

With me were two young men from Fall River (Mass.) who had been slightly bitten with the lure of the North. I also had a favorite niece of mine along, and we planned to accompany the party as far as Sydney on Cape Breton (Island) and there wish them bon voyage. The cruise in the cramped quarters of the schooner was a rather strenuous one for my niece, but she still treasures the experience and considers herself a real survivor of an Arctic expedition.

She and I returned to my home in Vermont to watch my father slowly wasting away. On the day of his funeral I received a letter from one of the Fall River fellows aboard the *Lilly of the North*, stating that she had been piled up on the rocks well down the Labrador coast, and her cargo was a total loss. They were going inland for a little hunting and fishing and would give me the harrowing details on his return to the States. I never knew if Jensen ever received his supplies. If he ever got wind of the fact that I had anything to do with the expedition, he might infer that I had something to do with the shipwreck for his refusing to give promised help to Shaw and myself two years before—that is, if he had a guilty conscience.

[1] There is no written account of this journey among the Porter Papers, RG 401 (27–B).

[2] See chap. 3, p. 33.

[3] This may have been Sam Bartlett (see chap. 2, p. 22). The Bartlett family included his cousin Moses, who served as mate on Peary's seventh polar expedition, 1905–6; his nephew Robert, who served as skipper in charge of that expedition and the one in 1908–9; Harry, who was master of the *Falcon* during Peary's second Greenland expedition; and John, who was master of the *Hope* on Peary's 1896 and 1897 summer voyages to Greenland.

Peary as we found him at Etah in 1900

Peary's home in 1900

Chapter 6 1899

THE SUMMER in Frobisher Bay, described in an earlier chapter, had turned out a failure so far as the work I had planned was concerned, but it pointed the way to another visit to Greenland, viz., by organizing another party of students and inducing Peary to land us on the northwest coast.[1] Webb Waldron, in the *Saturday Evening Post*, has referred to these parties of mine as "dude outfits" by means of which I not only secured a fine summer's outing for myself but paid off my entire college debt amounting to over a thousand dollars. Perhaps the members might take exception to being put in the dude class, but, as to the rest of the statement, Waldron was quite correct. As I remember now, the per capita expense for each "dude" was $600, and a few ads in the college papers soon located the six fellows glad of the chance. It led them into a quite inaccessible region abounding in big game and inhabited by a tribe of Eskimos living virtually in the Stone Age.

I made all the arrangements with H. L. Bridgman, the secretary of the Peary

[1] Although the heading to this chapter is 1900 in the typescript, the chapter relates to Porter's 1899 journal. In addition, with the Porter Papers, RG 401 (27–B), is a U.S. flag on which the following is sewn: "Presented by the Ladies of 'The Evergreens' to the North Greenland Hunting Party *S.S. Diana* Peary Expedition 1899."

Porter's account of this relatively short expedition is recorded in a looseleaf notebook, pp. 5–26, which contains three pencil sketches of the headlands of the central west coast of Greenland bearing the date July 97, and the maximum and minimum temperatures for July 31. The date of the first entry in the Journal, p. 7, is "Saturday 5th Aug 99"; the last entry, p. 25, is dated "Sept. 12, 1 P.M." Undoubtedly, these loose sheets are a record of Porter's short association with the Peary Arctic Club's 1899 relief expedition in the *Diana* (see chap. 4, n. 14). The *Diana* was sent to rendezvous with Peary's ship, the *Windward*, in order to resupply his expedition, to urge him to return to the United States for treatment of his frostbitten feet, from which some toes had been amputated, and to engage in seal hunting for next winter's dog food. The resupply mission and the seal catch were successful, but Peary did not abandon the expedition. Among the Porter Papers is an unpublished manuscript entitled "Walrus hunting or getting dog food for Peary." It refers to the ships' rendezvous and to the seal catch for the winter of 1899–1900. Porter's Journal of his 1898 expedition (see chap. 4) contains entries regarding his voyage on the *Diana*.

Arctic Club.[2] Peary himself was then in the far North, hammering away at the Pole, and the ship was to carry supplies to him and bring back the news.

The voyage north was uneventful. We presented our respects as usual to the governor of Greenland at Disko, probably leaving him a crate of oranges as a special mark of courtesy, dropped two parties at Nugsuak (Nugssuaq) and Upernavik for geologizing, and then entered the dreaded Melville Bay. This indentation on the west coast has been a bugbear, more or less, to arctic explorers. There are a number of enormous icebergs filling it, the product of the greatest glaciers in the world.[3] There is also a shifting, treacherous ice pack. However, she smiled on us and let the *Diana* pass through in a record run to Cape York, an outpost of the most northerly people on the globe, the Whale Sound Eskimo. Just around the cape is the sound itself—peopled there with perhaps a hundred natives—and here we were to pass the summer.

[2] See chap. 4, n. 14, and Helen Bartlett Bridgman, *Within My Horizon* (Boston, 1920), and *His Last Voyage, Herbert Lawrence Bridgman, 1844–1924* (Brooklyn, 1924).

[3] This statement probably is no longer true because detailed exploration and aerial photographic reconnaissance have revealed large glaciers, such as the Beardmore Glacier, in West Antarctica. See, for example, the following folios in the Antarctic Map Folio Series published by the American Geographical Society and edited by Vivian C. Bushnell: Folio 2, *Physical Characteristics of the Antarctic Ice Sheet* (1964); Folio 7, *Glaciers of the Antarctic* (1969); and Folio 12, *Geologic Maps of Antarctica* (1969, 1970). For an excellent terrain map of Antarctica, see the polar stereographic projection published by the American Geographical Society of New York at a scale of 1:5,000,000 at 71° south latitude. For articles on glaciers in Antarctica, see M. E. Giovinetto, "The Drainage Systems of Antarctica: Accumulation," *Antarctic Research Series*, 2 (1964), 127–55; "The Antarctic Ice Sheet," *Cold Regions Science and Engineering I–BI, U.S. Army Cold Regions Research and Engineering Laboratories* (1961), pp. 1–50; and Laurence M. Gould, "Glaciers of Antarctica," *Proceedings of the American Philosophical Society*, 82 (Philadelphia, 1940), 835–77.

At Cape York the kayakers came off to the ship.

Before the ship left us to make contact with Peary farther north, there was instituted a great walrus hunt to provide the commander with winter food for his dogs. We found them—the walrus, or is it walruses?—lying on the ice pans north of Herbert and Northumberland islands.[4] The technique of the chase was as follows:

You sight the quarry looking like so many red maggots asleep on the floating ice pan. The ship stops, puts over the boats armed with rowers, gunman at the stern, an Eskimo in the bow with his harpoon and float. You creep up cautiously on the quarry until discovered and then begin to shoot. If lucky, one or two are left dead on the pan. The rest flounder into the sea, mad as hatters, and come up all around the boat bellowing. Then comes the excitement, for those walruses want to get their tusks over the gunwale. The Eskimos go crazy, yelling and beating a tattoo on the boat. The man at the stern is firing indiscriminately now to frighten the herd away. Pretty soon they sound—all disappear, only to come up some distance away.

Now begins the chase proper. You can't get a walrus in the water by just killing him; he will sink and be lost. That's why the fellow is in the bow with his harpoon, line and float attached. He bides his time, makes his throw, takes a turn of the line around the forward thwart, and off we go—tearing through the water while the gunman waits for his coup de grâce. There's only one spot that's vulnerable, the backbone at the base of the brain. Anywhere else, the bullet simply plumps into

[4] See Porter's Journal, 1899, p. 7, and his unpublished manuscript "Walrus hunting" among the Porter Papers.

Take your time, old man.

several inches of blubber. After the animal is shot, he sinks, of course. You signal the ship, she steams up, lowers a tackle, and the steam winch hoists mister walrus over the side with his ton or two of blubber and drops him into the waist with a jar that shakes the ship. If there's no ship handy, as with our party later, you row to the nearest ice pan and, with a native-made tackle, warp him out of the water onto the ice, cut him up, load the boat, and make for camp.

The Eskimo knows well the secret of multiplying power much the same as we apply the block and tackle.[5] He reaves his line of walrus hide through the back of the walrus and through a hole cut in the ice, and with several heaving on the line the job is easy enough.

[5] See Boas, "The Central Eskimo," in *U.S. Bureau of American Ethnology, Sixth Annual Report, 1884–1885* (Washington, D.C., 1888), 399–669; *The Eskimo of Baffin Land and Hudson Bay* (New York, 1901–7); and "A Year among the Eskimo," *American Geographical Society Journal (Bulletin)*, 19 (1887), 383–402.

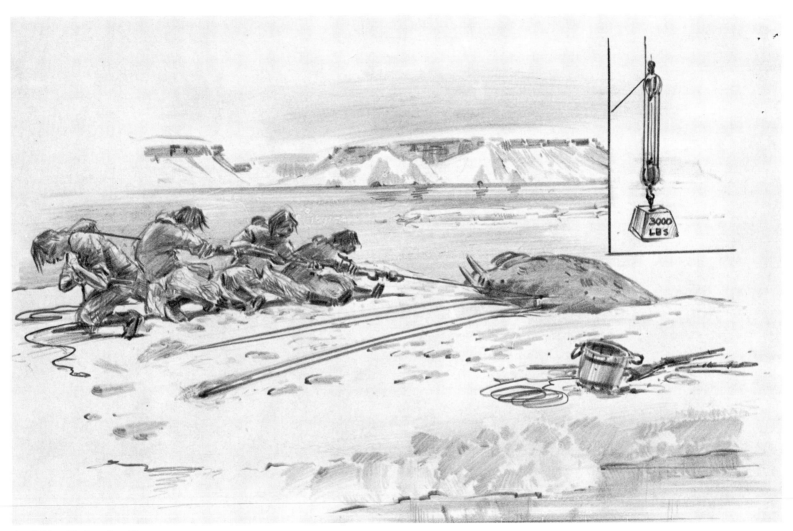

An Eskimo block and tackle

The first walrus we got in this way. After he was hauled up, the natives went straight for his stomach. Its contents proved to be clams or mussels laboriously shelled by the animal for food. They were considered a great delicacy among the natives. But although some of the party tried them, I couldn't bring myself up to the point of experimenting myself. Later, in Olriks Bay, the Eskimos did the same thing; that is, on killing a reindeer, they went for his stomach. Here, the stuff was fermented reindeer moss, which looked exactly like spinach. But I can't tell anybody if it tasted like spinach, for I didn't try it.[6]

When the men were fed up on walrus hunting, the *Diana* came along and landed us at the lower Narrows part way up Olriks Bay, for reindeer.[7] Before leaving our camp on Herbert Island let me tell of the mica mine I found there.

As I was roaming over the rocks a mile or so from camp, I came across the stuff strung along the surface in a seam a hundred feet long or so. I broke off a slab about a foot square, stowed it away in my bag of dunnage, and on the return to Boston looked up the president of a large mica concern. He slid his knife under a thin layer, tore it off, and held it up to the light.

"Look there, and there, and there." And he indicated with the knife blade some tiny spots of a rusty color. "Those specks are iron. That rules it out for use as an electric insulator, where most of the mica today finds its market. It could be used as windows in stoves, but the demand would not warrant the cost of mining it at such a distance." And so the mica mine went aglimmering, like the gold mine in British Columbia.

[6] For a discussion of Eskimo foods and eating habits, see Vilhjalmur Stefansson, *The Friendly Arctic: The Story of Five Years in Polar Regions* (New York, 1925), 230–34 and 355–56.

[7] See Porter's Journal, 1899, pp. 9–11.

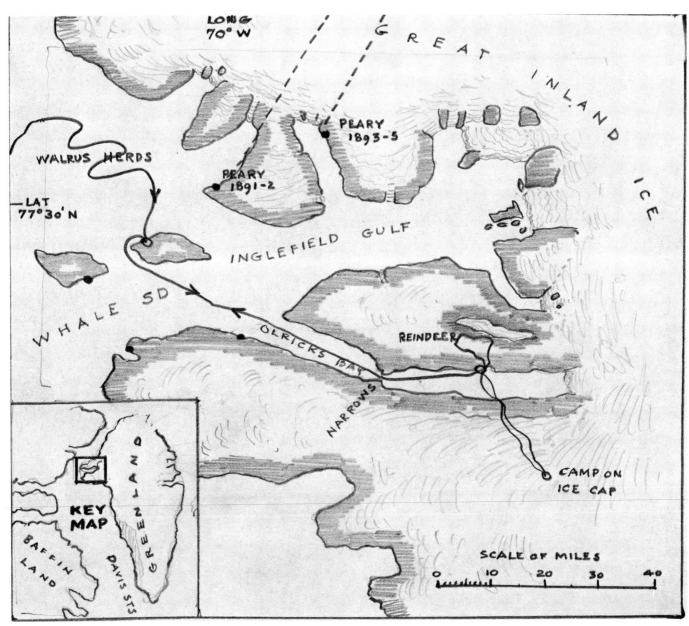

LONG
70° W

GREAT INLAND ICE

WALRUS HERDS

PEARY
1893-5

PEARY
1891-2

LAT
77° 30' N

INGLEFIELD GULF

WHALE SD

OLRICK'S BAY

REINDEER

NARROWS

CAMP ON
ICE CAP

KEY
MAP

BAFFIN
LAND

DAVIS STS

GREENLAND

SCALE OF MILES

0   10   20   30   40

The Whale Sound region, northwest Greenland, showing the
track of the "dude" outfit.

Myu—Chief

Kiota, son of the chief

From the camp in Olriks Bay, Shaw and I went out for caribou.[8] We took along old Myuksoah, the chief of the tribe. Somewhere among the mountains, Myu showed me a sort of runway between two cliffs where in years gone by, before the advent of the white man, they drove the caribou through this pass and brought them down with bows and arrows. "Now the deer are all gone," he moaned. "White men come with guns. Shoot all the caribou." And he blubbered like a child. I knew that Peary had drawn heavily on the reindeer for food and clothing.

We had hunted for over two days when Shaw saw, and stalked, a buck and finally brought him down. Our hunger was so great that we ate raw venison before waiting to build a fire and cook it.

Back at camp, others of the party had secured fifteen reindeer. Leaving Shaw at the camp, we rowed across the fjord to where a likely ascent offered access to the great inland ice. The Eskimos had their sleds and dogs, and a day's travel into the interior found us on the cap with only a level expanse of snow clear to the horizon in all directions. No sign of land anywhere, nothing but the steel-blue shield of Greenland's great snow mantle. Here, camp was made for the night (although the sun never went below the horizon), and the following day we returned to the camp in the bay.[9]

I was greatly disappointed to have missed Lieutenant Peary, who had visited the camp during our absence.[10] Shaw said he was in fine spirits although limping from the amputation of several toes frozen the previous winter. He seemed quite sanguine about reaching the Pole the coming year.

It was not until April 6, 1909, about ten years later, that Peary achieved the dream

[8] For a description of this hunting expedition, see ibid., pp. 12–19.
[9] For a discussion of this short expedition onto the Greenland ice cap, see ibid., pp. 17–18.
[10] Ibid., pp. 18–19.

Eskimo woman and child—Cumberland Sound

of his life and reached the North Pole of our earth.[11] What admiration must we all feel for this American who spent his life for the sole purpose of reaching this goal. At one time in his work he frankly admitted that the scientific reward was insignificant and of no commercial value. He placed his effort on the simple plane of a sporting venture that called for the finest qualities of patience, persistence, and unflagging determination. Year after year he stormed the ramparts, only to be cruelly disappointed. His final reward was to be sadly blunted by the miserable Cook-Peary controversy that probably robbed him of a great deal of the acclaim he so richly deserved. As these lines are being penned, a ship is sailing north to erect at Cape York, the threshold of Peary's stamping ground, a monument to this great explorer.[12]

Back on the ship again, the summer well gone, we visited a few settlements. I left the old chief and his son most of my camping gear. Dirty, greasy, their bodies swarming with animal parasites. Nevertheless, kindly hearts were beating under their birdskin shirts. The *Diana* turned her bow southward, the demon of Melville Bay again opened and closed his doors politely, and this, my last trip to Greenland, came to a close.[13]

[11] For Peary's account of this achievement, see the Peary Papers, RG 401 (1), and his *The North Pole: Its Discovery in 1909 under the Auspices of the Peary Arctic Club, by Robert E. Peary* (New York, 1910). See also William H. Hobbs, *Peary* (New York, 1936), 352–68, and John E. Weems, *Peary, the Explorer and the Man* (Boston, 1967), 169–277.

[12] This monument is mentioned briefly in Hobbs, *Peary*, pp. 449–50. For additional information, see "Complete Documentary Record of the Peary Memorial Expedition, 1932," in the Mrs. Marie Peary Kuhne Papers, ca. 1920–1966, the National Archives Gift Collection of Materials Relating to Polar Regions, Record Group 401 (3).

[13] See Porter's Journal, 1899, pp. 19–25.

A.D. *1900 and still living in the Stone Age*

*Good-bye to the sun for 130 days. Our winter quarters in
latitude 81°48'N*

74

LET US PAUSE for a moment and strike a balance. Twelve years since the goddess first beckoned, twelve years out of my life, and where was I? Certainly not at the head of my profession. What had these six ventures above and under the Arctic Circle given of material advantage? Nothing. Each year I had returned to civilization to find my fellow workers forging ahead, while I again took up my pencil and leaned over the drawing board. Why couldn't I drop into the humdrum of city life and be contented like other people? I was now thirty, my life span well along. Good reason to pause and think it over.

Writing this at sixty, I freely admit that I was making a fool of myself.[1] Had I kept my nose to the grindstone, perhaps I might have arrived in architecture. But why try to reason with a fellow sick with arctic fever, for by this time, 1900, the call was apparently stronger than ever? These "dude parties" were child's play. I must have the real thing—a try at the Pole itself—and the opportunity came that very winter.

Reports of a big expedition were in the air. A man worth millions who believed money could find the Pole had been found, and his purse was open to an unlimited extent to whoever would undertake the job. The man worth millions was William Ziegler of New York, and his choice for commander was Evelyn Briggs Baldwin.[2]

---

[1] If Porter, who was born Dec. 13, 1871, was sixty years old when he wrote this narrative, then the account was written in 1930–31, when he resided in Pasadena, Calif.

[2] For Ziegler's biography, see *Dictionary of American Biography* (1936), 655–56.

Baldwin also was an observer for the U.S. Weather Bureau from 1892 to 1900 and a meterologist on Peary's north Greenland expedition in 1893 and on the second Wellman arctic expedition to Franz Josef Land in 1898–99, and he made a voyage to Spitsbergen in 1897. For his biography, see ibid., pp. 47–48. For publications by Baldwin about the Arctic, see "Auroral Observations on the Second Wellman Expedition Made in the Neighborhood of Franz Joseph Land," *Monthly Weather Review and Annual Summary*, Mar. 1901 (Washington, D.C., 1901); "Drifting across the Pole," *New York Herald*, Sept. 6, 1908, and June 27, 1909; "The Meteorological Observations of the Second Wellman Expedition," *National Geographic Magazine*, 10 (1899), 512–16; "Meteorological Observations," *U.S. Weather Bureau, Report of the Chief*, 1899–1900, pt. 7 (Washington, D.C., 1901), 349–436; *The Search for North Pole or Life in the Great White World* (Chicago, 1806); and a narrative about the 1901–2 expedition in *Wide World Magazine* (London), Jan.–Mar. 1903. His manuscript field notes of the second Wellman polar expedition, 1898–99, are among the Records of the Weather Bureau, Record Group 27, in the National Archives.

As Mr. Baldwin's efforts failed to attain the pole, he is almost better known now as the man who discovered Mr. Ziegler. Never before in the annals of arctic exploration had funds been placed without stint at the disposal of a pole-seeking aspirant.[3] All of them—Peary, Cook, Nansen, Stefansson, Amundsen—had barnstormed the public, lectured, written, and pleaded with philanthropists for the bare necessities of their calling. If men like these, with meager funds, could almost turn the trick, why shouldn't Mr. Baldwin, with millions at his call, bring back the North Pole and then go for the other one.[4] This surely was my chance, and I was soon enrolled as artist and surveyor to the expedition to be known as the Baldwin-Ziegler Polar Expedition of 1901.[5]

Baldwin's plan was to attack the Pole from the other side, from a small group of islands known as Franz Josef Land, an archipelago north of Russia. He had purchased the finest whaler of the Dundee fleet, the *Esquimaux*, rechristened her the *America*, and enrolled her in the New York Yacht Club. Each department was being organized on a grand scale. In addition to the *America* there were two auxiliary ships. One, the *Belgica*, was to land a house and stores on the west Greenland coast against our retreat in that direction; the consort, *Frithjof*, to carry three years' surplus food.[6] Of the forty members, there were six Russian dog-and-pony drivers and a crew of Scandinavians.[7] Siberia was combed for nearly five

[3] Ziegler made $250,000 available to Baldwin for outfitting and carrying out the expedition of 1901–2.

[4] Porter is referring to Antarctica.

[5] With the Porter Papers, RG 401 (27–B), are many of his artworks from this expedition, an inventory of these items, and the following records of his participation in the expedition: a partially bound log (1901) within which are various pencil sketches; a brochure entitled "Farewell Dinner to the Baldwin-Ziegler Polar Expedition, Hotel Marlborough, Thursday, May 23, 1901," including several pencil sketches or portraits; a blueprint of the *Midnight Sun*, Sept. 1, 1901, a one-page newspaper published in Franz Josef Land; a cache note, May 18, 1901, from Kane Lodge in Franz Josef Land; a pocket-size notebook bearing the inscription "Property of Russell W. Porter, Artist, Baldwin-Ziegler Polar Expedition, Franz Josef Land, Feb. 20, 1902."

[6] Of the three vessels used in establishing and provisioning a base, the *America* was considered the flagship.

[7] The six Russians were added to the personnel of the expedition in Archangel.

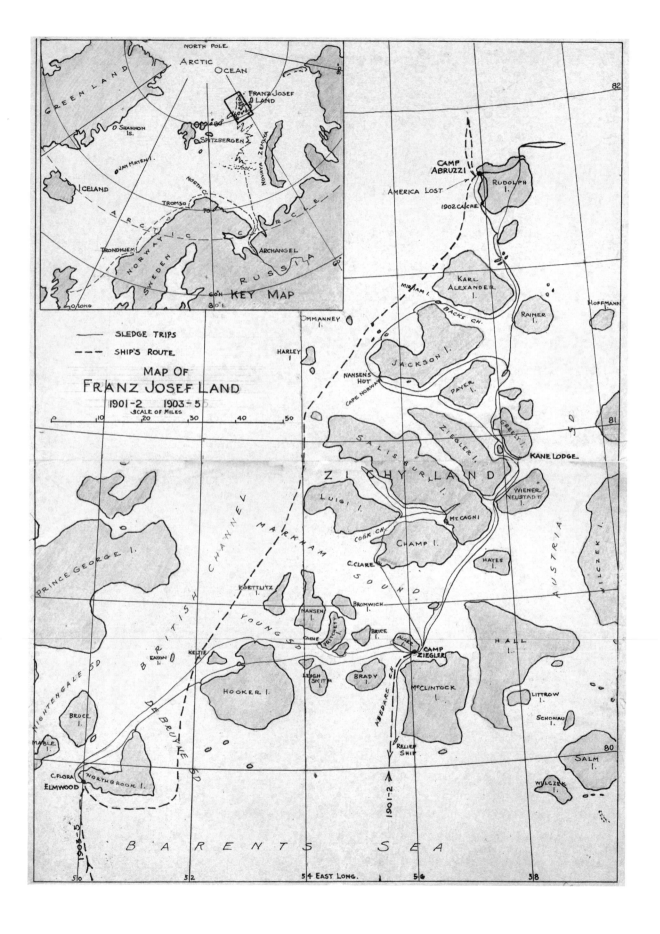

KEY MAP

SLEDGE TRIPS
SHIP'S ROUTE

MAP OF
FRANZ JOSEF LAND
1901-2   1903-5
SCALE OF MILES

hundred dogs, about fifteen Siberian ponies, and countless reindeer skins and Samoyed coats. Tons of pemmican, dog biscuit, dried fish, condensed foods, and compressed, baled hay. When we finally cut loose from Europe, the *America* looked like a floating haystack.

With Ernest DeK. Leffingwell, I was booked (second class) to Dundee, Scotland, where our ship was being outfitted.[8] I had a letter to the liner's captain asking permission to use my sextant while crossing the Atlantic. The captain turned me over to the third officer, and from then on I was either with him in his cabin or on the bridge. His name was David Pearson. The friendship persisted long after our return. Before leaving him at Glasgow, I had asked him to drop my mother a note. By sheer luck I took this same ship home in 1902 and found Pearson with half a dozen letters from my mother written up to the time of her death at Christmas when I was far away in the North.[9] They were filled to overflowing with love for her son, saddened by the conviction that she should never see him again. It is my one bitter pill, my sole regret, that this passion for the North should have brought sorrow to this dear woman.

While the personnel was arriving at Dundee, Dr. Verner, one of the surgeons, and I took bicycles and spent a glorious week in the Eastern Highlands of Scotland—Aberdeen, Balmoral, Glen Shee, Dunkeld, and Perth.[10]

Across the North Sea, up the Norwegian coast by the Lofoten Isles shrouded with the glamour of Verne's *Nautilus*,[11] across the Arctic Circle to Tromsø, then around the North Cape, and down into the White Sea to Archangel, Russia.

Archangel presented strange contrasts: log huts and squalor, with beggars everywhere, against fine homes and princely clubs. The banquet in our honor was lavish with choice foods and wines, presided over by the governor of the province

---

[8] For his autobiography, see "My Polar Explorations, 1901–1914," *Explorers Journal*, 39 (1961), 2–14.

[9] See p. 96.

[10] In the back of the pocket-size notebook that Porter kept on the 1901–2 and the 1903–5 expeditions are names and addresses, including one for a William W. Verner, 1136 Western Ave., Allegheny, Penn.

[11] Jules Verne, *Twenty Thousand Leagues under the Sea* (Boston, 1874).

Russians loading dogs at Archangel

and all the foreign consuls. It was our last taste of the fleshpots of civilization for over a year, and most of us made good use of the opportunity. Later, over the short commons of the trail, we lingered lovingly over memories of that feast.[12]

We were off at last. One thousand miles of Arctic Ocean separated us from the small group of islands known as Franz Josef Land. This part of the globe was unknown until Von Payer, an Austrian, ran across it in 1879, lost his ship and had to reach civilization in boats via Novaya Zemlya.[13] A good deal of the Barents Sea is cluttered with drifting ice; some of it navigable, some closely packed near the archipelago. We were negotiating it over a month before sighting land, waiting for leads to open up, some of which proved dead ends that required a return to open water and further trials. A landing was made at Cape Flora, a spot around which is centered a good deal of the history of the region. Here Nansen contacted the Englishman Jackson after the Norwegian's memorable drift across the arctic basin and sledge journey southward.[14] Then for us followed a desperate attempt to work

[12] See Porter's Log, 1901, pp. 21–30.

[13] Publications concerning Julius ritter von Payer's expedition and the discoveries made include his *L'expédition du* Tegetthoff; *voyage de découvertes aux 80–83 degrés de latitude nord* (Paris, 1878), and *New Lands within the Arctic Circle: Narrative of the Discoveries of the Austrian Ship* Tegetthoff, *in the Years 1872–1874* (London, 1876).

[14] The penetration of the ice-strewn Arctic Ocean to Cape Flora in Franz Josef Land is described in Porter's Log, 1901, pp. 37–43. For a brief history of earlier explorations, including the meeting of Nansen and Johansen with Jackson at Cape Flora and their departure on the *Windward* for Norway, see Frederick G. Jackson, *A Thousand Days in the Arctic* (New York and London, 1899); "The Jackson-Harmsworth Polar Expedition," *Geographical Journal* (London), 4 (1894), 141–47; "Three Years Exploration in Franz Josef Land," ibid., 11 (1898), 113–38; and *The Lure of Unknown Lands: North Pole and Equator* (London, 1935).

The summer ice pack

north between the islands for a high latitude in which to winter. Only the descending polar night called a halt and forced us into winter quarters on a southerly island called Alger, ten degrees from the Pole. All the channels were jammed with ice. Once, the ship ran aground.

The site chosen for the quarters was a flat area on the south side of the island, with the *America* anchored a hundred yards off shore. Portable eight-sided huts were erected where the Russians lived. A stable sheltered the ponies, and the dogs were strung out on long stake lines outside. The remainder of the expedition lived aboard; a daily routine was laid down for all of us, and we settled down for the long night of more than a hundred days.[15]

[15] In his Log, 1901, pp. 47–51, Porter describes the scene and the site settled on Alger Island.

Baldwin-Ziegler Expedition, August 8, 1901

To harden the men for the spring sledding and to become familiar with driving dogs, Mr. Baldwin instituted a series of trips to the other end of the island, bringing back loads from a cache landed there earlier in the fall. It was during these trips that the first dissatisfaction with the commander arose among some of the men. The distance to the cache was not far—perhaps eight miles—but the trips were made in darkness, and it wasn't long before two parties were lost, and relief parties brought them back in rather bad shape, with feet and fingers frostbitten. They naturally asked for sleeping bags or tents, perhaps both, in case it should happen again in the drift storms that come up so suddenly in the North. This the commander refused, giving as his reason that the added load would mean that much less freight could be brought back. Many of the fellows were put "on the mat" and reminded of their signed agreement to obey their commander under any and all conditions. The outcome has gone from me for the present. Perhaps it was a compromise. Nevertheless, from then on the seeds of discontent were sown. Leffingwell, the chief scientist, complained (and with reason) that his work was suffering from inability to carry on his observations, as he was continually hauling freight.

The winter dragged along, however, as it is wont to drag in the Arctic. Mr. Baldwin with the Russians established an advance post at Kane Lodge on Greely

Frozen in for the winter

Island, fifty miles north.[16] Shortly after, with the return of the sun, every available man, dog, and horse was drafted for hauling supplies northward. As a result of the season's sledding, several tons of food and equipment were landed on Rudolph Island, the most northerly of the group, only to be picked up by Fiala in 1903 and carried to his winter quarters a few miles farther on. There would be something almost humorous in this vagary of fate were it not for the heartbreaking drudgery expended on dragging that stuff over hundreds of miles of ice.[17]

Strange to say, Mr. Baldwin left me much to my own devices, and as artist to the expedition I was here and there with my team, trying to record the high spots of the country and the events that were transpiring.[18] On our return the following fall, Mr. Ziegler, on hearing that Baldwin had retained all my artwork, saw to it that my drawings, paintings, and notes were returned to me. There surely was enough happening along the freight route to keep me busy. Life on the trail, dog fights, getting around water holes, making camp and breaking it—always plenty of action. The region too had its charm in form and color.[19] On the return of sunlight after a hundred days of lamplight, the entire snowscape was enveloped in a lavender tint that persisted for several weeks. I had never heard this mentioned before, but it was quite apparent, and my suggestion was that the eye, so long robbed of sunlight, was supersensitive to the blue end of solar light when it at last returned.

West of Kane Lodge near Coal Mine Island (I discovered coal here two years

[16] Greely Island was named for Adolphus W. Greely, commander of the U.S. Lady Franklin Bay expedition, 1881–84, and Kane Lodge, on the southern tip of Greely Island in about latitude 80°57'N and longitude 58°20'E, for Dr. Elisha Kent Kane, surgeon-scientist on the U.S. first Grinnell arctic expedition, 1850–51, and commander of the U.S. second Grinnell arctic expedition, 1853–55.

[17] Porter describes this drudgery in his Log, 1901, pp. 74–111.

[18] See n. 5.

[19] See Porter's unpublished manuscripts, 1901–2, "The Brilliant Coloring of the North" and "Sketching under Difficulties, or the Trade of an Arctic Artist," in the Porter Papers.

The through freight. Sledding supplies north

later) my companion Andrée and I found a water hole and, near it, several walruses sleeping on the fast channel ice. They were tame enough. I could prod them with my alpine stock and they would only grunt in disapproval at being disturbed—quite different from our experience in northern Greenland when hunting them in open water. I obtained some fine close-up photographs, the first to be taken of these animals in their winter habitat.[20]

Out in Markham Sound one day while stormbound under the lee of an iceberg, someone suggested we kill a little time trying out the possibilities of dog meat as a diet.[21] There happened to be a dead dog outside. He was soon dismembered and in the pot. My recollection now is that the feast was not a great success. Peary, in recounting his starvation period on the great ice cap, refers to dog as rather tasteless, but to me it was decidedly "doggy."

[20] These photographs are among the Porter Papers.

[21] The voyage of the *America* into Markham Sound in early September is recorded on pp. 61–62 and 70–71 of Porter's Log, 1901, while the only reference to dog meat appears on pp. 79–80.

Walrus

A ton and a half of dog food

One of my side trips, however, got me into trouble. I was sketching the shoreline of a new channel west of Collinson Channel.[22] The men were asleep in camp some three miles away. I was so engrossed in my work that I didn't see the bear until it was too late. I made myself as small as possible behind an ice hummock, but he discovered me and, with a bear's customary curiosity, ambled up for a closer look.

Yes, I had a gun with me, but it wouldn't work. Each time I pressed the trigger, the hammer moved down slowly and rested on the firing pin. Later investigation showed that the oil had congealed in that temperature (-35°F).

Well, what to do? I remember dropping the gun, pulling out my knife, and beginning to yell and dance. This did not have the desired effect on the bear, as bruin pricked up his ears and started towards me. I'll never forget his ears. They seemed enormous, as big, in proportion, as a rat's ears. It is rather strange that my memory is blank as to just what happened then. What I do remember was being on the camp side of the bear, slowly backing off and watching the bear smelling my knife and sketchbook. When he looked up and saw what I was doing, he started after me, and for the second time in my life I tasted copper.

All this time I was cocking the hammer and pulling the trigger—to no avail. Then I noticed that the trigger guard did not close up against the gun stock (it was a Marlin, the action is similar to that of a Winchester rifle). Striking the guard over my knee, I pulled again, and off the gun went, the bullet going through the bear's belly and the gun kicking me in the stomach. She bit at the wound, wheeled around and made down the shore while I, knowing now what ailed the mechanism, threw in another cartridge and dropped the animal a hundred yards or so away. In the excitement of the scrimmage my mitts came off. There was a fresh wind blowing up the channel; when I looked at my hands, the fingers were as white as alabaster. The simile is good. A frozen member looks exactly like alabaster—hard, brittle, and semitranslucent.

I have told this bear story hundreds of times, and everybody knows how a bear story takes on added thrills at each telling, but I can only offer my diary written then

[22] In his Log, 1901, pp. 70–71 and 81, Porter describes his sketching, surveying, and mapping activities, his inability to capture the beautiful colors of the Arctic, his problem with freezing watercolors at Cape Teggethoff, and his decision to abandon pastels and oils when he "had tried selecting the pastel colors on deck but found it impossible for lack of light and did so in the studio under the incandescent lamp; it looked all right then, yes, but people don't generally look at pictures in color under an electric light."

The bear was smelling
of my sketch book

and the testimony of Mr. Baldwin, who visited the spot soon after.[23] I met him walking out from camp.

"Good evening, Mr. Baldwin, did you hear shooting just now?"

"No. Why?"

"I just shot a bear down the channel."

"Well, we'll go back to camp, hitch up a team, and bring him in."

Which we did.

"You needn't take my word for it, Mr. Baldwin," after describing the adventure and as we approached the scene of the fracas. "There is the whole story right there on the snow—footprints, blood, bear—everything."

On the way to camp I asked to have the skin of that bear and was refused. All I have to remember of the affair is the bear's jaws, which I chopped off the head after the dogs had eaten the meat and torn the skin to pieces.

There seems to be some question as to whether a polar bear will voluntarily attack a white man. The governor of Umanak, Greenland, once told me of an Eskimo hunting at a seal hole through the ice. The bear came up from behind and got his claws into the fellow's back. Somehow the Eskimo got hold of his gun, pointed it over his shoulder and shot the bear. The fellow's back was covered with scars.

However, I am just as well pleased not to have had to prove or disprove the theory. You may be sure that thereafter I saw to it that my rifle was always in working order.

As a result of Mr. Baldwin's policy of concentrating on advancing supplies north, the year yielded little to science. With virgin land all about us, no one was allowed there. It was forbidden ground. As a result, Leffingwell produced only a meager traverse of the region bordering the freight trail. Since then, Leffingwell has done fine work by himself clearing up unknown territory on the north coast of Alaska. Year after year he has left his home in sunny California and, alone, with a meager outfit, cleared up several thousand square miles that were blanks on the chart. His work has been incorporated in the government maps. Little time was lost, on discovering we were living in the same place, Pasadena, in getting together and talking over old times. On such occasions Mr. Baldwin's ears must have burned.

[23] Porter does not include this episode in his Log, 1901, in which the last entry is dated Jan. 26.

The artist at work

The pendulum apparatus loaned by the government for gravity determinations remained unused.

As the summer wore on, a large windbreak of canvas was erected back of the Russian huts, a hydrogen generating plant installed, and several balloons inflated and set loose. It must be remembered that there was no radio in 1902; we were quite isolated from the rest of the world. Suspended from the balloons were strings of buoys that were freed automatically as the gasbag descended to an earth, ice, or water surface. Each buoy contained a message, and several of them have since been recovered—one only this year (1931), on the shores of Novaya Zemlya.

About this time there was a rumor that the commander was signing up some of the men to remain over winter while the ship returned to civilization to prepare for

Messages to the outside world

another attempt the following year. As no diaries were allowed to be kept, my memory is a little hazy on the point. An attempt was made, however, to free the ship for a return home. Dynamite was used to blast out a channel through Abedare Channel, and it was not long before we felt the welcome heave of the ocean beyond the margin of the ice. I say "welcome." Everyone was anxious to get home.

When the ship arrived at Tromsø, orders were given to allow no one ashore. The captain, Johansen, with whom Baldwin had had trouble, took French leave over the side. The ship was in a filthy condition, fairly alive with human parasites, so the rest of us felt justified in following the captain. Here, at Tromsø, in a letter from an old friend, Ozora Davis, I received word of the death of my mother, who dropped from heart failure as she was ascending the stairs of the elevated in Chicago on Christmas day.[24]

Verner and I spent a leisurely month journeying down through Norway and Sweden to Stockholm, crossing to Göteburg by canal. A week in Copenhagen, where I revisited an old Greenland acquaintance in Jutland,[25] a day in Edinburgh to see the astronomer Royal Copeland, who had once visited Franz Josef Land, and then New York.[26]

This, my first fling at the Pole itself, was rank failure. But even so, within a month of our return I had signed on for the reorganized expedition as assistant scientist.

[24] See p. 78.

[25] See chap. 2, pp. 24–26.

[26] This very likely was the astronomer Ralph Copeland, whose publications include several concerning Franz Josef Land. See *Dictionary of National Biography*, Supplement, vol. 1 (1927), for a brief biography of Copeland.

Blowing ourselves to
a way out.

ON THE COMMANDER'S RETURN to New York that fall, and after Mr. Ziegler had received all the facts of the previous year's work from various members of the expedition, Mr. Baldwin was peremptorily removed from command. Curious to know who would take his place as head of the second expedition, I anxiously awaited the mails.

Said Professor Despradelle, "Eh bien, monsieur l'explorateur! Will you now get down to architecture? Have you had enough of the North? We have many interesting projects to design. Allez, donc, to the drafting board."[1]

Then a letter from Fiala. "I've been chosen. Will you go with me?" The goddess of the north beckoned hard, and I replied that I would.[2]

Anthony Fiala—all explorers now know Fiala, who outfits parties to all quarters of the globe. Fiala had been the official photographer to Baldwin and had made a clean job of it, bringing back a fine photographic record of the year's effort.[3]

[1] See chap. 2, n. 1.

[2] Among the Porter Papers, RG 401 (27-B), are the following records that refer specifically to the 1903–5 Fiala-Ziegler polar expedition: a copy of "The Arctic Diary of Russell W. Porter during the Years of 1903–1904–1905, While a Member of the Ziegler Polar Expedition to Franz Josef Land. Anthony Fiala, Commander"; a pocket-size untitled diary for the years 1903 and 1904 that has been modified and from which sheets have been removed; a copy of an incomplete, untitled typescript of diary notes, July 26–Nov. 13, 1903; and four reports from Porter to Fiala—July 13, 1904, on his trip from Camp Abruzzi to Elmwood, Franz Josef Land, between May 9 and July 13; Apr. 27, 1904, covering his trip with Anton Vedoe between Mar. 27 and Apr. 25; Mar. 20, 1905, on the spring sledge trip, Cape Flora to Teplitz Bay, Feb. 18–Mar. 17; and Mar. 25, 1905, for the period ca. September 1904–Mar. 25, 1905.

[3] The commander of the second Ziegler arctic expedition was Anthony Fiala, whose qualities of leadership had been significant in holding the expedition personnel together. For his biography, see the *National Cyclopaedia of American Biography*, 38 (1953), 53–54. His publications about the expedition include "Speech by Anthony Fiala at the Annual Dinner of the National Geographic Society," *National Geographic Magazine*, 17 (1906), 22–37; "Polar Photography," ibid., 18 (1907), 140–42; and *Fighting the Polar Ice* (New York, 1906).

Fiala was a skillful photographer. In 1913 Porter and some other members of the Fiala-Ziegler expedition received from Ziegler's secretary an album of selected photographs taken by Fiala.

Fiala photographing

Everybody liked Fiala. He informed me that the scientific work would be under the auspices of the National Geographic Society with William J. Peters (of the Geological Survey) in charge. Mr. Peters would also be second in command.[4]

Nearly all the old men wanted to go with Fiala. He had plenty to choose from. In one respect, the personnel differed from the previous year. It was to be 100 percent American. The crew and ship's officers were old whaling men from around New Bedford (Mass.). There would be no Russians. The route north would be as before, via Europe and Franz Josef Land.

I was told to try to improve on the cookers which had proved unsatisfactory. It must have puzzled the neighbors on Beacon Hill (Boston) to see the iceman in the dead of winter continually leaving large quantities of ice at West Cedar Street, where I was experimenting.

By May (1902) I was crossing the pond again, this time to Liverpool, Newcastle, the North Sea, and Bergen. The *America*, reconditioned, was at Trondheim, Norway's ancient capital. From here I journeyed alone around the North Cape to Archangel for furs and clothing, hunting for an astronomical instrument called a vertical transit, lost in the shuffle the year before. The party began arriving in twos and threes. Picking up our old dogs at Tromsø, we took on more in the White Sea, more ponies—we said good-bye to the world near Hammerfest. With one or two false starts we found the right lead through the pack and soon raised familiar landmarks over the northern horizon. Cape Flora was revisited and a message left at Jackson's hut that all was well.[5] Then a determined drive at the British Channel for a high northing.

The gods were certainly with us here. Day after day, little by little, the pack moved

[4] Peters was chief scientist and second in command on the Fiala-Ziegler expedition. His immediate staff included Porter, first assistant scientist; Robert R. Tafel (Philadelphia), second assistant scientist; Francis Long (Brooklyn), weather observer; and John Vedoe (Boston), assistant. Examples of publications by Peters are *Scientific Results Obtained under the Direction of William J. Peters, Representative of the National Geographic Society in Charge of Scientific Work* [on the *Fiala-Ziegler Polar Expedition, 1903–1905*], ed. John A. Fleming (Washington, D.C., 1907; and "A Reconnaissance in Northern Alaska, by F. C. Schrader, with notes by W. J. Peters," *U.S. Geological Survey, Professional Paper*, No. 20 (Washington, D.C., 1904), 1–139.

[5] In the southwest corner of Northbrook Island at the southwest entrance to Franz Josef Land.

The America *by moonlight*

away from the land and allowed the *America* to squeeze through. By September we were at the most northerly tip of Europe—Rudolph Island[6] —nothing beyond but the floating polar pack, clear to the Pole. Everyone aboard was jubilant. The northing wrested from the ice gods the year before by so much travail was now covered comfortably. Landing at the Baldwin cache, we took it aboard and proceeded around a headland into a rather shallow bay to what proved to be winter quarters.

Here five years before, the duke of the Abruzzi, nephew to the king of Italy, had wintered and with sleds reached at that time the farthest north, a few miles beyond Nansen's record.[7] Evidence of past occupancy was noticeable ashore—a large tent where the Italians had been forced to live when their vessel had been forced up on the beach, a large cache of food boxes on a pile of rocks. Beyond, the rising snow dome of the island; to the north, west, and south, the shifting ice pack. An extensive raised beach overlooking the bay offered a place to dig in for the winter. A house was to be erected there, also the circus tent to shelter the animals, while the ship was to be occupied by the crew.

The bay was not much good as a harbor; it hardly indented the coastline. More sheltered places had been found among the islets farther south, but at the first intimation of the ship's leaving us, such a protest arose from those who were to remain ashore that the commander decided, I am sure against his better judgment, to dock the *America* alongside the fast, old ice filling the bay, with no protection from north and west—and from which anchorage she was destined never to leave.

However, ere darkness descended all was snug and tight for the long winter months. When the house was completed, electric lights were installed, supplied by cable over the bay ice from a generator aboard ship, where steam was to be maintained in the boilers. Down near the shore, away from any trace of iron, Mr.

[6] Approximately in latitude 81°45′N and longitude 58°30′E. Rudolph Island is the northernmost island in Franz Josef Land.

[7] The duke of Abruzzi (Luigi Amedeo), Italian vice admiral and explorer, organized an arctic expedition in 1899 for the exploration of Franz Josef Land. Capt. Umberto Cagni of the expedition left Camp Abruzzi in the northwest corner of Rudolph Island and, using dog teams and assisting parties, reached latitude 86°34′N, Teplitz Bay, slightly nearer the Pole than Fridtjof Nansen was in 1895 (latitude 86°13′N).

CHRISTMAS GREETINGS –

from the PORTERS ·A·D·1939·

S·Y· America, Franz Josef Land, September, 1902.

Peters established the magnetic hut. In the opposite direction I built the observatory and set up the vertical transit.[8] By November darkness was upon us in earnest.

The first intimation to us on shore that all was not right on the ship came one night when the arc light in the living room went out. As I started over the bay ice several vague forms emerged. They were sailors. One of them, seaman Duffey, acted as spokesman.

"You see, Mr. Porter, the ice began screwing against the side of the ship until she began to rise by the bow. We don't want to disobey orders, but it's unsafe to stay aboard that ship, so we came ashore."

I went out across the bay following the cable. Aboard the *America* all was commotion. Caught between the fast ice of the bay and the relentless pressure of the pack, she was held between the jaws of a vise. Slowly under the terrific pressure her sides were being crushed in.

Somebody leaned over the rail far above me. It was the steward. "Look out below," he cried, and heaved down what looked like a gunny sack that crashed on the ice. The contents were flatirons and lamp chimneys. Laughable perhaps, but humor of a grim sort, as we watched our only contact with the outside world being ground to pieces. Too late now to reconsider a safer harbor. The ship was doomed with forty men marooned on the tip end of the old world, and no getting home without outside succor.

For several days the *America* seemed unwilling to give up the ghost. Held in her

[8] See Peters, "Section A. Magnetic Observations and Reductions," in *Scientific Results*, pp. 1–359, especially pp. 5–6, 13, 321, and 358, and Peters and Porter, "Astronomical Observations and Reductions," ibid., pp. 597–622.

The observatory

icy grip, I used to go out and visit her by moonlight. There is a striking moon photograph by Fiala of the ship's bow forced high in the air as in mute appeal for help. Great ice blocks had tumbled onto her deck. The engine room was half filled by drift. Plenty of time now to remove anything of value. Her cozy deck cabin presented a sorry spectacle after the walls had been stripped of their finish. Then an offshore gale completed the havoc. Nothing but a jumble of ice and small bergs and black water. The good ship was gone, sunk there at her berth or carried away with the pack. In either case she left no trace.

Living quarters for the ship's officers and crew had to be provided ashore. An annex to the house was built, even a blacksmith shop and machine shop. Tunnels and passageways burrowed through the snow, filled with supplies. The living room was a hive of activity preparing for the spring campaign. Some of this work might have been done in the States, but it is the policy of arctic venturers to keep all hands busy in one way or another through the long night. No idle hours for sea lawyers or nail keg orators.

My diary notes that the esprit de corps after the loss of the *America* still ran high. This was shown by the keen anxiety of the men as they waited for the final orders from the commander announcing the personnel for the polar dash, each one of us jealous of his rights and hoping to be in that last small group to stand on the Pole.

Just before she was crushed

For myself the winter passed quickly. There were the chronometers to wind and compare daily. At the observatory, through the vertical circle, I held vigil with the stars, watching the pinpoints of light moving over the cross hairs of the telescope and recording the transits by wire on a chronograph at the house. The purpose of much of the astronomical work was to ascertain how the chronometer clocks were behaving, whether they were gaining or losing, and if so, how much. The layman little realizes how important a knowledge of Greenwich time is to the seeker of the Pole. It is the only means of deriving his longitude. For longitude is nothing but time expressed in degrees and is always the difference between the time at Greenwich, England, and the local time of the observer.

As shown in the diagram, assume you are looking down on the North Pole of the earth. If the time happens to be noon at Greenwich, with the sun directly over that meridian as indicated, and a fellow in Franz Josef Land finds by observation that his local time is three in the afternoon, he subtracts his local time (three hours) from the time at Greenwich (zero hours) and finds that he is three hours, or forty-five degrees east longitude. The same rule holds true for any time of day or for any location on the earth's surface.

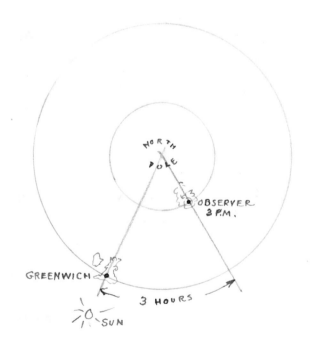

In the observatory

Now, the only way to carry Greenwich time—at least this was true in 1902 before the advent of radio; nowadays Greenwich time is to be had almost for the asking, by picking it out of the ether—is to transport it by a clock set to Greenwich time before leaving civilization, to be careful not to let the clock run down, and to check its daily rate by star observations.

The weak point in this theory, for us, lay in the rough usage our chronometers received during the voyage north. Using her bow for a battering ram, the *America* had charged the ice for hours. The shocks were enough to knock a man off his feet if caught unawares, surely unkind treatment to delicate timekeepers. And during this interval, observations were impossible.

There are other ways of finding out what time it is at Greenwich, however. The predicted times of celestial signals are given in Greenwich time in the nautical almanacs for years ahead. For instance, the time of disappearance of a certain star behind the dark edge of the moon on a certain date is given in the book; if you note the phenomenon, you have recovered Greenwich time.[9]

Of special interest to us was our dependence on G.M.T. (Greenwich mean time) in finding our way back from the Pole, for, as mentioned before, all directions there are south, and it became necessary to know which rib of the umbrella to come down on if we wanted to hit our headquarters.

Those were cold, cheerless hours at the observatory. No thrashing around to restore circulation. No shutting out the wind that had free access through the wall and roof shutter openings. There were times when the kerosene lamp refused to burn. The oil was like so much snow slush. Mercury could be molded into plastic shapes. Caught once by drift, I waited for hours, not daring to find my way to camp. Only the arrival of my bunkie Long with a lantern released me from confinement.[10]

One had to look twice at Polaris to notice that it was not quite overhead. We were eight degrees from the Pole, and the North Star was the same distance from the zenith.

There were wonderful nights of aurora. Like incandescent streamers, they

---

[9] These almanacs have been compiled for many years and published by the U.S. Navy Hydrographic Office in Washington, D.C.

[10] See n. 4.

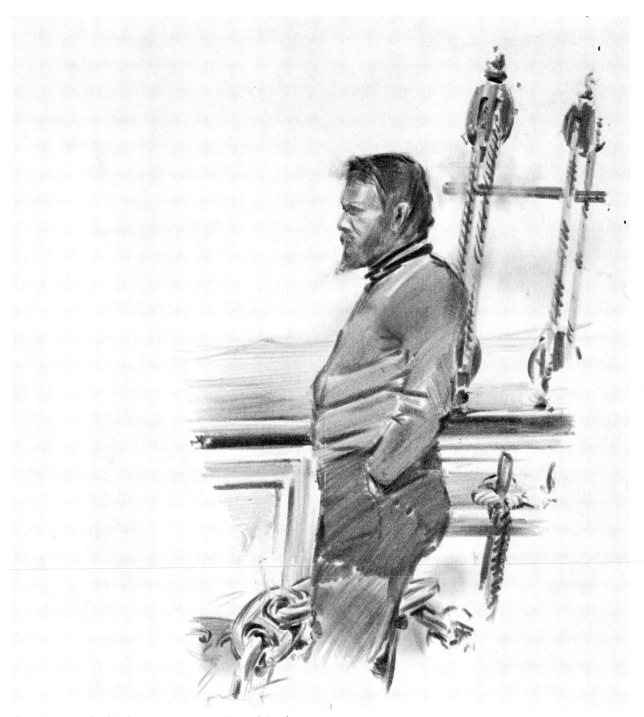

Serg. Long, my bunkie, last survivor (except General Greely himself) of the fated Greely Expedition

squirmed across the heavens lighting up the snowscape to almost full moonlight. Another display was the radiating arch near the horizon. At times faint iridescent colors marked the displays. At no time have I heard the sound of rustling silk accompanying auroral displays—frequently referred to in old accounts of arctic expeditions.[11]

The cold at minus sixty-two (our lowest) is little different in feel than minus twenty; that is, if there is no wind. But with the slightest air movement the lower temperature is immediately apparent, and it behooves one then to seek shelter.[12] Of the many attempts to protect the face, none were successful. Any object placed over the face soon froze to the skin. While most of the men let their beards grow, they removed all hair from around the lips. A common sight was to see one fellow come up to another and inform him politely that his face was frozen. A handful of snow held in the hand until it was slush was then applied to the white spot, with no more lasting effect than the skin peeling off some days later.

Meanwhile, Mr. Peters' assistants were making observations at the magnetic hut at two-minute intervals throughout the winter. As iron of any kind within fifty feet of the hut was taboo, these fellows, unlike myself, were unable to have a gun handy in case a bear became too curious. On one occasion John Vedoe heard bruin outside the canvas walls snuffing around.[13]

"I lifted the dip circle carefully off its pedestal," he told me, "and placed it on the floor in one corner so it wouldn't get hurt. Then I grabbed the deflection bar and thus with the decks cleared for action awaited the bear. I was looking for him to come down through the canvas roof, but he didn't and after awhile moved off."

The only compromise possible was a gun installed as near as magnetically

[11] For a brief description, notes, and sketches of this phenomenon, see Fiala, "Section B. Notes and Sketches of the Aurora Borealis," in *Scientific Results*, pp. 361–68.

[12] There are examples of various wind-chill charts related to the development of polar clothing in the Paul A. Siple Papers, 1905–1965, in the National Archives Gift Collection of Materials Relating to Polar Regions, Record Group 401 (4).

[13] See n. 4.

Pressure ridges

prudent—say forty feet away—but I don't imagine John felt any particular comfort in the thought.

Then there were hours sewing reindeer suits, diary writing, working up star sights, and listening to Long describe those days at Cape Sabine where the Greely party, one by one, died of starvation until about a third of their number (twenty-five) were left when relief arrived.[14] He recounted the killing of the bear that saved the survivors and the secret councils that resulted in the shooting of Private Henry for stealing food, and indignantly denied the practice of cannibalism. "Just a newspaper yarn," he said.[15]

[14] Sgt. Francis Long (see n. 4) had been a military member of the Lady Franklin Bay expedition, 1881–84, under Lt. Adolphus W. Greely. See the records of the Lady Franklin Bay expedition, 1881–1886, in Records of the United States Weather Bureau, Record Group 27, in the National Archives.

[15] For details of this incident, see Adolphus W. Greely, *Three Years of Arctic Service: An Account of the Lady Franklin Bay Expedition of 1881–84 and the Attainment of the Farthest North*, 2 vols. (New York, 1886). See also, in the National Archives Gift Collection, Record Group 200, the papers of David Legge Brainard, who was a member of the three-man unit ordered to execute Private Henry by a firing squad.

Peace Point, Northbroom Island, August 17, 1904

WITH THE NEW YEAR'S FESTIVITIES over, the sleds packed with food, and camp equipment in the dugout, the hour approached for the big getaway. The sun was returning; there was sufficient light for a day's run. Finally, the long cavalcade crept like a worm up over the ice dome of the island, following a line of flags that marked the trail.

It was an inauspicious beginning. Going into camp near the ice foot, we remained stormbound two days, only to be ordered back to headquarters. Sleds broken down, stoves out of order, six of the men unfit for the work. It was more or less a shock, but back we went, made the necessary changes and readjustments, and started again, this time camping out on the sea ice perhaps a mile from shore. The end of the run had seen much rough ice and a lot of chopping to let the ponies through. That night Fiala called me into his tent where I found Mr. Peters and the man in charge of the dogs, Vaughan.[1]

"I have called you in on an important matter. Dr. Vaughan tells me that the sledges are going to pieces. This upsets my schedule. It may be the wise thing to go back now to headquarters and with improved equipment make another effort a year hence. Have you any suggestions?"

Mr. Peters was noncommittal. As I remember, he expressed himself as unqualified to give an opinion, as his department was science. However, he would abide by the commander's judgment. I know I came out flatly against going back, didn't believe that Mr. Ziegler or the world at large would consider that we had made an honest effort. The thought of turning around now after years of preparation, to turn tail when still in sight of land—the idea was unbelievable.

There were more arguments, pro and con, and I went to my tent. Later Fiala came to me.

"Porter, we have decided to give up the dash for this year. It's hard, but my better judgment tells me it's best."

---

[1] Dr. J. Colin Vaughan, an assistant surgeon with the Fiala-Ziegler expedition. Dr. George Shorkley was the surgeon, and Dr. Charles L. Seitz, another assistant surgeon.

The going was rough.

"Well," I replied, "all right, but give me a man and dogs and let me go on a few days and see what the ice looks like. It seems a pity to lose this chance of studying the pack."

"Good, and while you're out here, try to get to White Island, where the men that the duke lost were headed.[2] Perhaps you may find some clue as to what became of them, and possibly also of Andrée's fate.[3] And while you're at it, go on down among the islands and examine all the caches laid down by us and by Baldwin, for there will be a retreat to Cape Flora this summer and I have the responsibility of getting a lot of fellows, who are unfit for this kind of life, back safely to civilization."

In the dumps an hour before, I was elated now and picked my companion—Anton Vedoe.[4] He stood head and shoulders above any other man in the party for the work at hand. Shipmate on the Baldwin trip, Vedoe had always made clean-cut work of any job entrusted to him. He was a good dog driver, kept his equipment in efficient working order, and above all had an even, buoyant temperament. He too was overjoyed by release from the now disgruntled crowd.

Perhaps we noted an alacrity with which many of the party, on hearing the news of the retreat, broke their tents and harnessed up their dogs. It seemed but a short hour before they were again seen toiling up the dome of the island, headed for warm bunks and hot meals.

"A good riddance," remarked Anton as we entered our silk tent for a cup of

[2] Duke of Abruzzi, Luigi Amedeo. See chap. 8, n. 7. For details of Amedeo's 1899–1900 expedition, see his *Expedition de l'Étoile polaire dans la mer Arctique, 1899–1900* (Paris, 1904); *Farther North than Nansen, Being the Voyage of the* Polar Star (London, 1901); *On the* Polar Star *in the Arctic Sea, with the Statements of Commander V. Cagni upon the Sledge Expedition to 86°34′North,* 2 vols. (London, 1903); and *Die Stella polaire im eismeer: Erste italienische nordpolexpedition, 1899–1900* (Leipzig, 1903). See also J. N. L. Barker, *A History of Geographical Discovery and Exploration* (London, 1948), especially pp. 467 and 473.

[3] See Svenska Sällskapet för Antropologi och Geografi, *Andrée's Story: The Complete Record of His Polar Flight, 1897, from the Diaries and Journals of S. A. Andrée, Nils Strindberg, and K. Fraenkel, Found on White Island in the Summer of 1930* (New York, 1930); and *En ballon vers Pôle; le drame de l'Expédition Andrée, d'après les notes et documents retrouvés a l'ile Blanche* (Paris, 1931).

[4] Anton Vedoe and Porter conducted a significant planetable mapping reconnaissance of Franz Josef Land from Cape Flora to just beyond Rudolph Island and back. For a brief reference to this trip, see Porter's "Arctic Diary, 1903–1905," pp. 43–45, with the Porter Papers, RG 401 (27-B).

Upended like the dorsal fin of some monster

coffee. "Ain't it nice and quiet here? What a relief from the crowd." We could faintly hear the shouts of the dog drivers as they urged their animals up the glacier.

After a few hours' sleep, camp was broken and we followed a northeasterly direction for the rest of the day. The going surely was bad. Here on the exposed north end of the island, with nothing between it and the Pole but floating ice, there was but one huge pressure ridge after another. What little advance we made was over a chaos [sic] of huge upended blocks with deep soft snow between them. If only this zone of screwed-up ice that showed so plainly the influence of the nearness to land could be penetrated, there would be a chance of better traveling. When Captain Cagni left Rudolph Island four years before, he took to the pack directly in front of our winter quarters and over young smooth ice, and was well away from land when he came up to the old ice.[5] Not so here. We were surrounded on all sides by ice conditions that permitted only a mile or so northing for a day's effort. We worked over to a particularly high ridge and climbed to its crest to pick out the next day's run, but found only the same jumbled mass clear to the horizon—east, north, and west. As I scanned that abomination of desolation, it left a picture back in the cells of my memory that has never been effaced. A few years ago, about thirty years after the scene I have been describing, I was at work at the eye end of one of the world's largest telescopes, drawing the craters of the moon.[6] The ghastly white expanses of the lunar surface seemed startlingly near, due to the magnification of the powerful instrument. The similarity of this moonscape to the snowscapes of the North was enough to transport me back again to the tip end of the eastern hemisphere, looking out over the frozen polar sea. Throughout those nights at the

[5] See Amedeo, *On the* Polar Star.

[6] Porter became a member of the executive and the design and planning staff that was organized at the California Institute of Technology in Pasadena, Calif., in 1928, to build and install a 200-inch telescope on Mount Palomar. His official title was associate in optics and instrument design. For examples of Porter's engineering and artistic talents, see his sketches in James S. Fassero and Porter, *Photographic Giants of Palomar* (Los Angeles, 1948). Porter's contributions to Palomar are described on p. 4. For his drawings of moonscapes, see his "Moonscapes," *Popular Astronomy*, 24 (1916), 515–16 and plates 32 and 33. The original manuscript drawings of these moonscapes are with the Porter Papers.

With good going, traveling was a joy.

eyepiece I was not in sunny California; I was back in the Arctic under the cold light of a midnight sun gazing at the scarred surface of the shifting pack, the long lines of pressure ridges, and the sharp pinnacles of distant icebergs. The illusion was complete.

"It's no use, Vedoe. It would take a month to reach White Island. I don't know but what Fiala did the right thing to pass up this sort of going. There's no knowing how far it extends. We can put in our time to better purpose by looking up the food caches. Fiala's got some job on his hands getting that crowd to a relief ship. If the ship doesn't show up, those caches will certainly become popular."

There was not much conversation while moving. Each one of us had to give his undivided attention to his own team. Although we had good dogs, the sleds were heavily loaded and required careful maneuvering to prevent capsizing or jamming. From time to time there would be a movement of the ice blocks. One fault that was followed about a mile had a series of smooth, new ice areas, perhaps formed the day before.[7] Saltwater ice is always soft and slushy. There was a continual crunching sound, and occasionally an ice block would topple over.

When we finally reached the island and made camp a little way up the glacier, it began to blow and held us prisoners for three days. There is little use in trying to travel in the drift. Not only is it impossible to see where you are going, but the dogs dislike it. And, of course, if it is head-on, there is no alternative but to seek shelter. Drift storms are not snowstorms, for it is not snowing at all. As the wind increases in force, the loose snow is picked up and carried along with the wind. This layer of drifting snow gradually increases in thickness until you are completely submerged in it. Then, of course, all landmarks disappear.[8]

But in the tent, hot pemmican under our belts, snuggled down in our sleeping bags, with pipes going, we remarked on how comfortable we were and thanked our lucky stars we were not at headquarters. The tents were drift tight; that is, with canvas floor sewed to the walls and an entrance door made like a cloth tube with a pucker string, no snow could get inside. There was more or less loose hay on the floor. And on striking the tent when loading up, nothing was taken out. The whole

---

[7] Reference here is to a geological fault or a break between two blocks or masses of ice.

[8] This condition is called whiteout, often a fateful polar phenomenon.

Old faithfuls

123

affair, rolled up, was lashed to the sled. Of course, there were times when the tent grip gave way under high winds, but we didn't seem to mind it much. The collapsed tent lay upon us, drifts accumulated, and so we lay until the blow was over. Still, there's nothing like a snow hut of the Eskimo beehive pattern to weather out a storm in, as I found out the next year.[9]

The going south among the islands along the line of food caches was good, and when the going is good, sledge travel in the North is a joy. Smooth, fast ice joined one islet to another, and over this royal highway we made fast time, opening one cache after another, noting their contents and restowing those that had been damaged by bears. At Kane Lodge, erected by Baldwin two years before, there was the luxury of a stove and the chance to dry out our equipment.[10] Spring sledding in the Arctic is not all a bed of roses. The sleeping bags slowly absorb moisture until they are as stiff as dry hides, and it requires considerable time and patience to worm one's self into them and to thaw them out by the heat of one's body. This drawback to arctic comfort seems inevitable. Each time the bag is occupied, a warm object (one's body) comes into contact with a cold one (the bag). Moisture is therefore condensed on the colder one—the bag. As this goes on day after day, the bag gets heavier. The same thing happens to one's socks, although here the moisture comes mostly from perspiration. Each night they lay like wet compresses over our chests to dry out. Our boots, the Lapp Finskàs, were made from the legs of reindeer, which have the property of shedding snow. Inside these boots we placed handfuls of swamp hay called sennegrass. These false soles act as insulators against cold and absorb the perspiration from the feet. Each morning this perspiration is shaken out of the sennegrass like so much fine snow. The grass crumbles away with time and must be replenished.

The return to winter quarters was marked by a few high spots of interest. At the first camp we discovered coal up the side of a cliff on the west side of Coal Mine Island (called so afterwards).[11] This was considered an important find now that the

[9] An experienced person can make this type of shelter in a relatively short time from local materials and compacted snow.

[10] See chap. 7, n. 16.

[11] This discovery is mentioned in Fiala's "Introduction," in *Scientific Results*, pp. v–vii.

Coal Mine Island—coal was discovered here (see cross) several hundred feet above sea level.

ship was gone, and a fifty-pound bag was taken along for the ship's engineer to test out.

As Cape Norway lay near our return route, we visited the historic spot so that Anton could see with his own eyes where Nansen, his fellow countryman, had hibernated like a bear through a long night.[12] We found the remains of the hut in the same condition as when visited by Baldwin two years before. Bear and walrus skeletons strewed the beach, ribs protruding here and there through the snow.

The day before, there had been a bear scrimmage. One of the dogs had been thrown high in the air but, save for a slight tear in his side, seemed none the worse. But that night at Nansen's hut his head began to swell up until it was twice its normal size—it was a horrible sight—and the poor fellow was soon put out of his agony.

The next day we discovered an islet not on the charts. It was not much of a discovery as discoveries go, but it happens to be the only piece of new land I have been able to name. It is a huge pile of rock in the middle of Backs Channel and bears the name of Miriam; its only history as far as I know is as the site of a cold lunch and an uncomfortable head wind.[13]

Later that day we scrapped with a bear but lost him.

Meanwhile at headquarters some apprehension was being felt for our safety. The time presumed necessary for our scouting trip was long past. The commander had sent out one search party, which reported that there was little hope for us ever showing up. This report so worried Fiala that he took the steward and a dog team and started down through the islands. I shall never forget the day we ran across them. It was like finding a needle in a haystack.

Happy as larks, Anton and I were making fine time over the channel ice south of Hohenloe Island.[14] Only the stern duty of having to show up at headquarters and render our report kept us from extending the trip indefinitely. Well, there was more field work coming, and we were hoping to be thrown together again in the next shuffle.

"I see a tent."

"Where?"

"Look!"

Search as I would, nothing but ice and distant land.

[12] The southwest coast of Jackson Island.

[13] Miriam Islet, a tiny rock island that lies at the western entrance to Backs Channel.

[14] This island lies between Rudolph and Karl Alexander islands in about latitude 81°35′N and longitude 58°30′E.

Here Nansen had hibernated like an animal.

"There." And he pointed to a jumble of small rocks a mile away, where the small pyramid point of a tent could be made out silhouetted with the rocks against the sky. With full speed we dashed into camp and opened the tent flap.

"Good morning, everybody. Hello Fiala. Hello, steward. Ready for church?" For it was Sunday.

Fiala speaks of this reunion in the official narrative as one of his pleasantest recollections.[15]

"Yes, Porter, I was worried. The camp had long ago given you up. You know, the day after we left you out on the pack, there was a three-day offshore storm." (Those three days we were held snowbound on the glacier.) "The ice all went out, and it was feared you had gone with it. But somehow I believed you were down here somewhere, on the job."

"Well, I'm sorry, Fiala, to have made you this trouble. It's been nothing but a joy ride after we turned south. But it was just hell out there in the screwed-up ice. Perhaps your judgment was right in turning back. There was no hope in looking up traces of Andrée." (In 1930, when news of the finding of Andrée's body at White Island reached the world, it was thought at first that the discovery was made on the island that Vedoe and I had tried to reach. There was considerable publicity in the papers about our effort until it was found that the body was recovered in an entirely different spot; on White Island, to be sure, but distant from our White Island [Hoiden Island] by a hundred and fifty miles.) "There was no hope in looking up traces of the duke's lost men on White Island and at the same time finishing the work down here, which I assumed to be more important. What's the matter with those dogs?"

Outside was bedlam, as always when a bear shows up and there are any dogs around. Some of them were freed, and they soon had bruin treed on an ice hummock while we took time to go out after him. Then there was a morning service—Fiala was a very religious fellow—after which I took a round of angles and Anton sewed up a rip in his favorite dog's side where the bear had sideswiped him.

[15] See Fiala, *Fighting the Polar Ice*.

What three years of arctic fever did to Fiala

Altogether, the day proved a busy and a very happy one. And so we all made our way back to headquarters.

Spring had now arrived. The main program seemed to be to get the dissatisfied down to Cape Flora, where the relief ship was due in August. A staunch few were to remain here for another year's effort. With ample dogs and equipment, I was to run a traverse down through the islands and meet the commander at the ship rendezvous in July. There were three in my party, including Vedoe. Mr. Peters was to dismantle the observatories and bring the precious records south with an independent party.[16]

There is little to be found in this spring and summer trip to interest the general reader; it was quite uneventful; the usual scraps with bears, one day's run much like another, side excursions to vantage points where I could set up my plane table and tie up the topography within view. The theodolite was used to check our positions occasionally from sights on the sun, for it was summer now, with the sun above the horizon throughout the twenty-four hours; it was, of course, the only star in sight. As Elmwood was approached, a fine winter harbor for a ship was discovered on the north side of Hooker Island,[17] and here we stayed several days making a survey of the region and measuring the flow of a nearby glacier—the only active ice stream anywhere about. We dropped onto this beautiful spot from the ice dome of the island which had been crossed to save an area of rough channel ice. A near-tragedy occurred on this ice dome four months later when Fiala's party was returning north. Both he and the steward were precipitated seventy feet into a crevasse, from which they were recovered more dead than alive.

But advancing summer and the consequent breaking up of interchannel ice

[16] See Peters, "Section A. Magnetic Observations and Reductions," in *Scientific Results*, p. 14.
[17] About latitude 80°15′N and longitude 53°00′E.

Taking a time sight

warned us to be moving on if we hoped to make our destination. At Jackson's Hut at Cape Flora we found the commander and his party already arrived and well. They had put back the roof that the storms had blown from the hut and were living in it; that is, the ship's officers and crew were occupying it while the field and scientific staff were living in a small portable hut a hundred yards away. Behind the houses, the little auks were screaming in the cliffs above the talus; brooks were cascading down the mountain sides; birds filled the water lanes off the land. To the horizon stretched the shifting pack, and, as summer wore on and fall approached, anxious eyes scanned the distant scene for signs of a ship.

One day we tried a ball game under the cliffs. Above the screech of the birds in the rookery overhead, someone cried, "Ship," and the diamond was deserted. It was a false alarm, and before long serious attention was given to the possibility that relief would not arrive and, caught like rats in a trap, some provision must be made for the winter. I asked permission to establish a walrus camp a few miles away to collect as much dog meat as possible against another long night. At this camp we secured fourteen walrus, and with the first snows several tons were hauled to the settlement.

A coal seam had been found far up the side of the cliffs. Here the men toiled with what tools were available. Six tons of black diamonds were sewed up in walrus hides, rolled 700 feet down the talus, and sledded to the hut. It was a brown coal of inferior quality, but with a little wood it would burn. Several drift logs were located on the shores of the island and brought in. Of course, there are no trees growing in the archipelago, and these logs must have come from far-off Siberia, over a thousand miles away.

Finally, Mr. Peters and party arrived but without records or instruments.[18] It seems that he had preferred to travel without dogs, to cross the islands wherever possible, and to drag a canoe along against the possibility of open water. They had reached a small island (Eaton) well along in their journey when the ice broke up, and they were forced to wait for sufficient open water to use their canoe. Here they had cached their outfit and made a dash for Elmwood. They looked pretty well all in.

As darkness settled down on us, hope was definitely abandoned for relief from

[18] Porter's "Arctic Diary, 1903–1905," pp. 48–49, records the arrival of the Peters party (Peters, Tafel, and John Vedoe) as Aug. 31.

Cape Flora

the outside that year. The pack ice stretched unbroken to the horizon. It was probably a bad year for ice. It is just as well to say here, however, that two heroic attempts were made to reach us.[19] Each time, the relief ship used up her coal battering the ice and returned to Norway for more. Still, we hadn't the consolation of knowing even this. I knew it was going to be a disagreeable winter. While it is true that nothing succeeds like success, it is equally true on polar trips that nothing is so demoralizing as failure. Most of the crowd had had enough. They wanted to go home.

Leaving Long in charge, Fiala started back north again with a party of which I was a member. We reached the end of the island to find the British Channel still open, filled with shifting pan ice. There was nothing to do but dig in and wait until new ice formed. Three times we started out over the treacherous salt ice, only to be forced back. To kill time, we burrowed into the side of the glacier, carving out room after room. We called it the Tombs. Fortunately, a bear showed up that gave us dog food, but as the days went by I could see that fewer men would mean fewer mouths to feed. When I offered to return to the hut with any others and to meet him in the spring at Camp Abruzzi for the dash north, he seemed relieved, for the wait was fast becoming unbearable.

"All right," he said, "Take Jimmie, the cabin boy, with you. You are placed in charge at Flora during my absence. Meet me at Abruzzi, March 10. I shall wait for you until then."[20]

Back at the hut again, I found the party split into two camps. All available food had been divided. Each crowd was living independently of the other. I hadn't been in camp an hour before one of the men from "Little Italy" (the scientific staff so dubbed the duke's hut) accosted me.

"So you're in charge here, are you? Well, I don't recognize you, or Fiala either, for that matter. We're shipwrecked, we are, and all contracts are void. It's everyone for himself now."

With this attitude taken by men who should have known better (they regretted it later in the States), the prospects for a harmonious winter were not the best.

[19] Ibid., pp. 51–58.
[20] Ibid., pp. 57–59.

134

Feeding the dogs walrus meat

However, I bunked with the sailors, who seemed glad to see me, and waited patiently for returning sunlight.

The hundred days in that near-starvation camp (we were on less than half rations) would have proved a godsend to a writer who could portray with true dramatic sense the influence of the long night over the characters fate had thrown so closely together. Take the matter of food—and it was vile stuff, walrus meat that an Eskimo will eat only if he is starving. Now cut this food in half.

I quote here at length from my diary: "But you at home would be surprised if you tried it to see what a craving the flesh would feel should you stop eating before you had had what you wanted." The favorite topic, of course, was what we would eat if we returned to the States. The dream of the sailors, almost to a man, was a full meal of ham and eggs. The field department was more particular.

The most interesting character was, by far, the skipper, a weatherworn whaler from Edgartown (Mass.), wise about oil, grease, blubber, bone, and ships.[21] He did a good deal of his thinking aloud. I never got a word of it, and probably few of the sailors did. They were sort of stage asides.

The diary has him remark: "Guns? Rifles? Mr. Porter, how many rifles do you think I have bought and sold in my lifetime? I might say thousands. And as for walrus, I've seen them so thick you could not see anything else, thousands on thousands of 'em. But we never fool with 'em on our side [meaning Alaska]. Only Norwegians go walrusing, and they can live on almost anything. Why, these walrus here are nothing. I've seen, I suppose, tusks three feet long without any exaggeration, and yet there is someone thinks they can tell me something about walrus and how to shoot 'em. They don't know what they're talking about, that's all there is to that." On and on in this puffed-up strain.

Diary: "This morning when the captain took down his ham tin (full of snow water for washing purposes) hung up by the stovepipe, he found something in it which he had unwittingly scooped up along with the snow in the dark, something as big as my fist, and I would give twenty-five dollars to know who did it." I never saw him so

[21] Ibid., pp. 62–63.

The retreat south

wrought up with the world at large, ordering me to remove the matches from the wall over his table so that no one would have occasion to come into his corner.

However, someone did invade his corner in a hurry. The lie was passed between two sailors over in the other end of the room, and quick as a flash they came over, giving it to each other in earnest. When they arrived with a bang, over went my oil lamp, the covering over a window fell in, and down came the captain's table with its contents.

Now that we are on fights, here's another.

Diary: The skipper is sitting in his chair mumbling, delivering his usual asides, and the crew is conversing in low tones—some have disappeared into their bunks—when one notices loud talk down the passage by the kitchen.
"Look out now."
"Don't you touch me. I'm a sick man."
"You're no more sick than I am. Look out now."
"Bill Ross, if you should hit me now, I would drop like a dead dog. If you ever dare strike me, I will run this knife through your heart."
A quick, shuffling sound; an oil lamp tumbles to the floor sputtering in its spilt oil; a sound as of a man's wind being slowly cut off growing fainter and fainter until a sharp metallic ring is heard as the knife falls from relaxing fingers. A man emerges from the passage and throws a long sheath knife on the table in front of the captain.
"Dere, captain, you see, over six inches long—eight, if an inch. I've half a mind to run it into him now." And he makes a move for the knife but does not take it.

These pleasant little affairs at least had the merit of breaking the long monotony.[22] Monotony was there all right, for the next entry (December 21) says: "At last after days and days of waiting, this 'red letter' day has arrived. After all, it only means that the sun has stopped going down."[23]

There were consolation intervals with Long tramping back and forth across the frozen pond. He had been through it before at Cape Sabine with Greely, and he never seemed to worry.

[22] Ibid., p. 66, Porter mentions: "Finding time beginning to hang heavily on my hands, I have been of late making a 'polar' pack of cards, and a case to hold them, out of pieces of the lignum vitae sled runners, and inlaying it with ivory." Again, on pp. 91–92, he describes playing cards that he made for the crew. One of these much-worn, handmade cards is among the Porter Papers.
[23] Porter's "Arctic Diary, 1903–1905," p. 68.

The sun returns.

With the breaking of the winter's back, my thoughts centered on the trip I must prepare for, to meet Fiala 200 miles away by March 10. It didn't look too good. My dogs were reduced to four, and with ten days' food and equipment shaved to a minimum, it meant over a hundred pounds to a dog. Then again, I was hardly fit for severe exposure after so long a diet on short rations. Fortunately, a bear showed up whose skin provided me with a new pair of pants to replace those that were fast going to pieces.[24]

I picked as companion one of the five men (Vedoe being at Camp Ziegler) who had spent a winter among the Eskimos with Peary.[25] After several nights' practice, we were able to throw up a snow igloo in forty minutes. By the middle of February a period of calm days set in, accompanied by a full moon, and although the sun had not yet returned, I could not resist taking advantage of moon and weather to start north.

There was plain sailing for the first four days.[26] We realized at once the superiority of snow huts over tents, and although behind our schedule, the fifth camp found us forty miles from Elmwood, throwing up the igloo on the north side of Hooker

---

[24] Ibid., pp. 70–71.

[25] Ibid., pp. 94–95. The man Porter selected for his companion was the fireman G. D. Butland. For a brief account of this trip, see Porter's report, Mar. 20, 1905, on the spring sledge trip from Cape Flora to Teplitz Bay, in the Porter Papers.

[26] See Porter's "Arctic Diary, 1903–1905," pp. 95–98; his report, Mar. 20, 1905, on the spring sledge trip from Cape Flora to Teplitz Bay; and his report to Fiala, March 25, 1905.

Building a snow igloo

Island (not far from where Fiala had come to grief in the crevasse the fall before). But here, out of a clear sky as it were, my arctic goddess turned against me.

Drift poured down off the island like a veritable snowfall, slowly creeping up the sides of the hut until we dared remain inside no longer. Breaking out through the top, we went down along the shore ice and built another igloo, taking with us our bags and the dogs and leaving a ski stuck in the top of the submerged hut as a marker. The few hours of daylight prevented our digging out the sled.

The next morning we returned to the former campsite to find all traces of it gone, obliterated. Not a sign to indicate where the hut or ski was located, just a smooth slope of hard-packed snow. Our sled was covered at least fifteen feet, and the shovel was on the sled. They were two pretty solemn fellows that went down and into the second hut to brew a cup of tea and talk things over.

There seemed to be three alternatives. To retreat to Cape Flora.

"I'll be damned if I do," said Butland, whose sentiment I shared.

Then we could stay here and try to recover the sled, using a tin plate and skillet cover in lieu of the lost shovel, or we could push on somehow in hopes of finding a cache laid down by Baldwin two years before on a cape some thirty-odd miles away.

Diary: "It was the dogs that worried us—I mean their lives. You must remember that we had just emerged from an arctic winter, subsisting on half rations, and were in no physical condition to meet a severe test of staying powers."

Well, the last course was the one decided on. Our meager effects were laid out on the ice, and the knotty problem of how to transport them was tackled. Laying the two bags together with the food, fuel, and stove between them, the tent underneath to take the wear, the whole was securely lashed, with the front end bent up like a toboggan before it froze. At this juncture the goddess relented. Two bears, mother and cub, walking rapidly upwind between the pressure ridges, came literally into camp. One shot for the mother, two for the cub—Butland and I shaking hands and dancing a cancan at this great good luck that put danger out of the way for the present.

The few notes I jotted down give but meager information about the next seven days. It certainly looked like touch and go until we reached the cache and found the

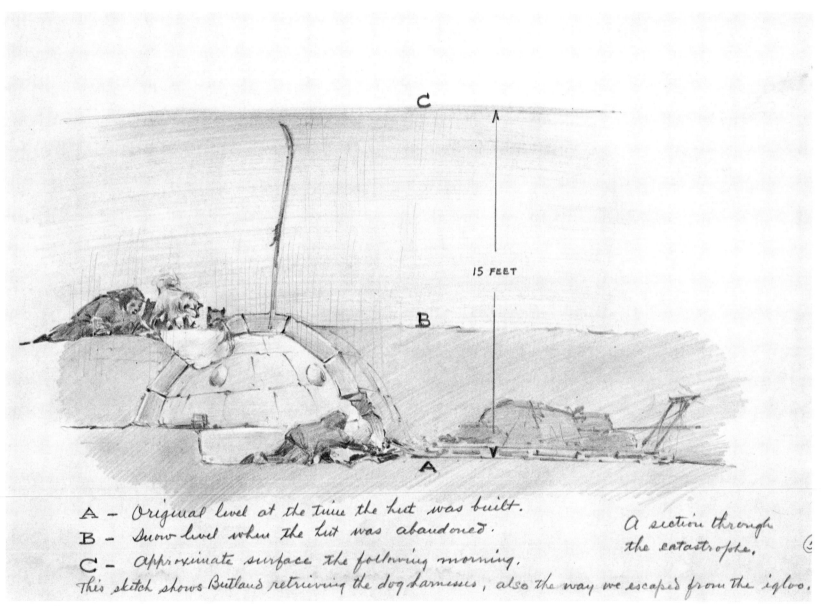

C

15 FEET

B

A

A – Original level at the time the hut was built.
B – Snow level when the hut was abandoned.
C – Approximate surface the following morning.
This sketch shows Butland retrieving the dog harnesses, also the way we escaped from the igloo.

A section through
the catastrophe.

A section through the catastrophe

143

corner of a box sticking through the snow. Turn and turn about, one of us would break trail while the other got into harness with the four dogs. There were deep soft snows. The unwieldy bundle dragged heavily. The last of the alcohol went the fourth day, and bear's blubber substituted. Continual frosting of my fingers made them useless, Butland having to do the lashing. Then his toes began to go.

The fifth day found us on an island within sight of the old winter quarters of the Baldwin expedition; that is, we could have seen it had it been clear weather. Here we were held prisoner two days by drift.

Diary: "P.M., March 4. As I feared, bad weather has caught us. We have made only three miles a day for nearly a week. Yesterday the whole afternoon was required to make something under a mile. But we hope for the best. Six of my fingers are badly blistered."

But the storm that held us in sight of our goal for two days had a silver lining. It packed or blew away the soft snow, making better going, and at the old West Camp we were furiously burning anything at hand to melt enough snow to quench our thirst.

It was an anxious moment as the old winter quarters at Camp Ziegler were approached. We were going to break through the roof if necessary, but such tactics proved unneeded. Certainly there was no expectation of finding living beings there. That was not on the program.

Nevertheless, there was a hole leading down toward the stable, with a gun and shovel lying beside it. My first thought was that the relief ship had reached here the summer before and left a party. But when I slid down the burrow and opened the door, there in the flickering light of a slush lamp were two begrimed familiar faces, the quartermaster's and a seaman's.[27] The ordeal was over.

Somewhere back on the long drag I made a good resolution. If ever I got through alive and back to civilization again, that arctic siren could go hang. I was done with her. She had tricked me once too often. Never again could she entice me back over the Circle. Stripped bare of all blandishments, she now stood before me a worthless conquest. The pledge has been kept—so far.

The rest of that trip was in sharp contrast to what had gone before. Butland with

[27] The quartermaster was Charles E. Rilliet; the seaman may have been Mackiernan, who replaced Butland when he left Camp Ziegler with a frozen heel.

Making dogs of ourselves

145

his frozen heel was replaced by Seaman Mackiernan, a new sled was found, and with light loads we made fast time up through the archipelago, arriving at our destination a week behind schedule. As our old quarters at Camp Abruzzi came in sight, the only sign of life was a solitary limping dog. Inside the house was one man, the old chief engineer.

"Fiala left for the Pole yesterday. He waited for you a week."

Even this news brought little regret.

The North is a hard taskmaster with its unforeseen setbacks and disappointments. To have my effort to join the commander come to naught by such a narrow margin as a day was a bit cruel. But the North is cruel and the lady herself heartless. Well, anyway, I'd done my best.

As matters turned out, it made little difference. The polar party was back in a week with the same old tale of impossible going—storms, open water, failure.

Everything now centered about the relief ship and a definite abandonment of further attempts at the Pole—to concentrate all souls at the southern end of the islands with the fervid hope that contact might be made with the outside world.

My party was the first to get away, followed by Mr. Peters with the scientific instruments.[28] The run down to Alger Island was uneventful.[29] Here, I built another astronomical observatory and set up the Repsold Circle. Peters continued the magnetic observations. Parties were now coming and going from Elmwood. The starvation camp had weathered the winter without loss of life. The expedition lost one man, a Norwegian seaman, Sigurd Myhre. He was found dead in his bunk at Abruzzi one day. The real cause of his passing was never fully known, as all the surgeons were at Elmwood, miles away at the time.

Coincident with Myhre's death was that of his wife in Bergen—to the very day.

There was an agreeable and profitable trip with Butland into an unknown region called Zichey Land that deserves a short description.[30]

That trip into Zichey Land with Butland was in some ways the most satisfying of

[28] See chap. 8, n. 4 and n. 8.

[29] Camp Ziegler was located on Alger Island, which is just north of McClintock Island in Markham Sound.

[30] An area of land that Baldwin thought he had seen but which Porter concluded was a series of islands and intervening channels. The name Zichey or Zichey Land does not appear on Porter's map of "Part of Franz Josef Archipelago."

Sigurd Myhre's grave

all my experiences in the North, for, to begin with, it was an ideal party in size—two persons—with none of the cross-purposes and bickerings that go with a crowd. Next, there was the thrill of being the first humans to enter this land. The goddess was to lift her veil at last. And last, Zichey Land proved to be one big nest of bears. Why, I can't say, unless our activities in other parts of the archipelago had led them to retreat into this untouched region for safety.

There was plenty of food on the sled and five good dogs. At the first camp in Markham Sound (Cape Clare) we bagged four ptarmigan, the first discovered in this part of the world and a new species.[31] At the second camp on the summit of a low glacier we looked down into the promised land but saw it vaguely through the fog. Here came the first bears, three of them. Can you picture it? Pandemonium among the dogs, rain, me in my stocking feet, Butland in his underwear—all staged on the upturned shield of that glacier. I had thought, while crawling into our bags after cutting up the first bear, that we would be left alone up here on the ice dome. Then the other two arrived.

My notes written at that time indicate that, when we were not stormbound, we were fighting bears. In a week's time the number had run up to sixteen. On the following day, crossing the new channel (Cook) there was hardly a moment without a bear somewhere in the snowscape. At the next camp three curious fellows kept Butland busy. From the brow of a headland (Mount Cagni) above the camp I watched the scene below through powerful glasses, my companion barricaded by the tent, sled and snowshoes, two guns at his side, watching a mother and her cubs as they hesitated between fear and curiosity.

Later, at Cape Farman, six bears were in sight at one time, most of them too near for comfort. I had an uncomfortable moment snarled up with the dogs, who had gone crazy, trying to stop a wounded mother who, badly wounded, was finally dropped among the dogs themselves.

Almost as vivid as this fight was the catastrophe of falling into a tide crack an hour later. It is no joke to fall into ice water up to one's middle at 20° below zero without a

---

[31] Cape Clare is at the extreme southwestern corner of Champ Island. For Porter and Butland's account of this trip, see Porter's "Arctic Diary, 1903–1905," pp. 109–14.

We looked down into a new land—islands, bays, and channels
slumbering under the midnight sun—never before gazed upon.
Here was recompense.

change of underwear. Streaking to camp, I disrobed completely and crawled into my sleeping bag while Butland hung up the soaked garments to freeze, the ice to be pounded out of them later. Fortunately I had been wearing pants of bearskin, from a bear shot at Flora the winter before. Bear fur has the property of releasing frost, snow, and frozen moisture when it is vigorously shaken.

Outside of all the excitement this trip afforded, nearly a thousand miles of unknown channels, bays, capes, islands, and glaciers were charted, the last of the archipelago to give up its secrets.[32]

All souls were now at Ziegler and Elmwood except Fiala and the old chief engineer. At last a party was dispatched north to find out if they had started south. The next day Fiala showed up with the chief, but too late to head off the relief.

As the summer wore on and no ship arrived, I found myself often looking across the flat to the meat rack, which seemed none too well filled. One afternoon, as July was coming to a close, Mr. Peters dropped into the observatory to go over with me how best to conserve what little paper we had through another year. A form darkened the doorway, and "Chips," the carpenter, appeared, holding aloft a glass bottle.

Diary: "Hello, Chips. Come in."
The bottle was placed on the table before us. It was half full, and I applied my nose to the opening.
"Why, it's beer," I exclaimed in surprise. "Where did you find it? And L. Macks Olbrygurie, Tromsø, too. Run across some old cache of the Baldwin expedition?"
"No, no; help yourselves."
I looked at him. The perspiration was standing out in big drops over his forehead, and he seemed to find difficulty in breathing. Surely, I thought, this fellow has been hitting it rather

---

[32] See the following publications written by Porter and included in *Scientific Results* for examples of his surveying and cartographic accomplishments, despite great odds, during his stay in Franz Joseph Land, 1903–5: "Section E. Astronomical Observations and Reductions," pp. 597–622; "Section F. Map Construction and Survey Work," pp. 623–30 and map; "[Map of] Part of Franz Josef Archipelago Surveyed by the Ziegler Polar Expedition, 1903–4–5. Scale 1:600,000. Surveyed and Drawn by R. W. Porter under Direction of W. J. Peters"; and "Map of Franz Josef Archipelago. Compiled from Surveys of the Ziegler Polar Expeditions, 1901–02, 1903–05. Scale 1:750,000. Surveyed and Drawn by R. W. Porter under the Direction of W. J. Peters."

Bears in camp

heavily. Nevertheless, I filled two cups and offered one to Mr. Peters.

"Well, anyway, here's to—to—the relief ship's coming this year." It was all I could think of worth a toast. Even then I couldn't understand.

"You don't understand, Mr. Porter, you don't catch on," the carpenter protested.

Then Peter's face began to change. Then, not until then, did the arrival of a ship enter my mind.

"Chips, the ship hasn't come?"

"Yes."

"Come, no joking."

"Yes, it has, it has."

"Say it again."

"The ship is at Cape Dillon.[33] The party is at the house now."

It was hard to believe even then, with so many rumors of ships about. With shaking hands, Mr. Peters and I drained the aluminum cups to the sand dregs and followed the carpenter down to the house. Turning to me, Peters smiled (he rarely smiled when with me) and said, "There's no need for economizing on paper now."

At the house there were some of our men from Cape Dillon, looking jaded and worn out

[33] At the far southwest corner of McClintock Island, about eighteen miles south of Camp Ziegler.

Man on an ice flow with his boat, 1907

from their hard trip up the channel. It was remarkably quiet, considering. But it was true, and soon Fiala himself came in.

"What ship?"

"*Terra Nova.*"

(I knew her by reputation, largest whaler in the Dundee fleet.)

"Go on."

"Mr. Ziegler is dead."

Another pause. The hush in the house now seemed perfectly natural.

"Go on, go on."

"Japan and Russia at war. Russia nearly wiped off the earth."

"Go on."

"Norway and Sweden about to go to war."

"Who is president?"

"Roosevelt."

"Tell us more."

"The *Reliance* won the cup," etc., etc.

On July 31, near high noon, Camp Ziegler was abandoned. The long cavalcade took up its march down Abedare Channel, over rotting ice mostly covered with water.[34] After twenty miles through thick fog came the wail of the ship's siren, then the loom of the ship. She looked awfully big to us. She also looked awfully good. From our position under her massive bow we looked up to face a shower of welcomes.

Aft in the saloon were comfort, luxury, and ease—music, books, cigars, wine—and, best of all, soft, new, clean clothing. Letters from home!

As the last frowning headland sank below the northern horizon, I fear my adieus to the arctic goddess were none too respectful. "What's that?" I might have said, shaking my fist in her face. "See you later? No, I'll not see you later. Good-bye, old girl. You've played fast and loose with me now for ten years and I'm done. Your promises have proved a delusion and a snare." These were not the words I used, but they expressed pretty well my feelings as the *Terra Nova* worked her way out of the ice into open water and pointed her old bowsprit towards Hammerfest. But there remained still a slight uneasiness, for I thought I detected something like a mocking laugh coming over the stern.

[34] According to Porter's map of Franz Josef Land, Abedare is spelled "Aberdare."

Mat Henson

Chapter 10   1906

I LANDED IN NEW YORK sick and sore at heart at the way the Goddess of the North had handled me. My head felt like a block of wood. At the Hotel Russell in London I had dined with Mr. Champ and Mayor Gaynor. Peters was there, Fiala was there, but I heard scarcely a word that passed over the board. Slowly it dawned upon me. My deafness, scarcely noticed in the wilds, had now assumed serious proportions. No one cared to shout in that dining room. Was this calamity, too, to be laid against the North? A specialist in Washington said no, that it was common enough among women. But my friends said, "See now what your obsession has brought you? We told you so."

That winter in Washington, helping Mr. Peters prepare our scientific results for publication, gave ample time to reflect upon my folly. The specialist suggested I stop smoking but compromised on a very mild tobacco—taken sparingly.

Among those on the dock to welcome us home was Dr. Cook.[1] He took me to his home in Brooklyn and unfolded a plan for conquering the highest mountain on the North American continent, Mount McKinley.[2] It was a wonderful prize, he said, almost to be had for the asking. He had tried to ascend it a year or two before but failed and thought he now knew how to turn the trick. His plans were almost completed and he needed a surveyor, for he was going into virgin country.[3] It lay just on the Arctic Circle, ten thousand miles away in the heart of northern Alaska. Would I like to go?

I asked him to tell me more. Well, there would be a lot of pack horses.

"I don't like pack horses, Doctor," thinking of those cayuses back in 1898.

[1] Frederick A. Cook, physician and explorer. See chap. 1, nn. 5 and 7. For biographical sketches of Cook, see *Dictionary of American Biography*, Supplement Two (1958); *National Cyclopaedia of American Biography*, 13 (1906), 338–39; John E. Euller, "The Centenary of the Birth of Frederick A. Cook," *Arctic Journal*, 17 (1964), 419–21; and Russell W. Gibbons, *Frederick Albert Cook: Pioneer American Polar Explorer* (Hamburg, N.Y., 1965).

[2] Cook later wrote a book about his climb to the top of Mount McKinley. See p. 162.

[3] Porter received a series of letters from Cook asking that he favorably consider appointment as topographer-surveyor on Cook's Mount McKinley climb. This correspondence—Mar. 9, 14, and 29 and Apr. 1 and 28, 1906, and three undated letters—is with the Porter Papers, RG 401 (27-B).

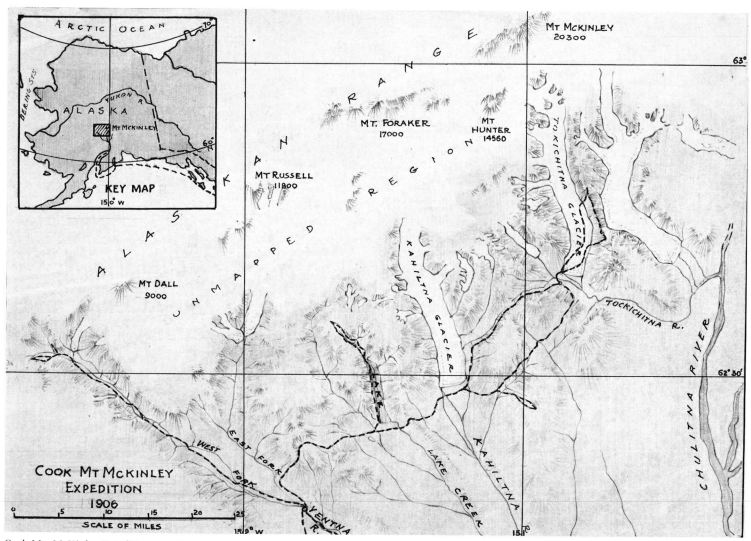

Cook Mt. McKinley Expedition, 1906

157

"But there will be experienced packers to take care of them. And then there's a forty-foot power boat with a powerful Lozier engine in it to get up the glacial streams."

That sounded better.

"Yes, I'll go. It will probably be my last fling at the North, but I'll go in spite of the mosquitoes. I can still hear her calling."

There were only a few in the party.[4] Prof. Herschel Parker from Columbia, Belmore Browne, artist, and the packers whom we would pick up with the horses. There was the long ride across the plains. The horses were herded into a freight car at the Yakima Indian Reservation, and we were in Seattle boarding the steamer for the North.[5]

Juneau, Sitka, Valdez, Seward, and, at last, Cook Inlet with its smoking volcanos.[6] As the steamer was landing our supplies, I could see in the dim distance the tiny white silhouette of the snow-covered Alaska Range. It must have been 150 miles away. Somewhere in that jumble of peaks was the top of the continent.

The packers started off at once with the horses—overland to meet the boat and supplies at a given rendezvous. With the *Bolshoy* loaded to the gunwale, we started up the Susitna and Yentna rivers. The streams were large, swift, and full of shifting bars, over which the power boat was able to navigate, for her screw revolved in a tunnel formed on the underside of the hull. So loaded was the water with sand and silt that we could hear it like rustling silk as it rubbed the boat's bilge.

In no time at all, a few days only, we had made contact with the pack train. Here the range stood out against the northern sky in all its grandeur. Directly ahead was a sag in the skyline that indicated a pass, and to this we made our way, leaving the boat

[4] Among the Porter Papers are the following documents that relate directly to Porter's association with the Cook expedition to Mount McKinley, 1906: a diary—pp. 1–6 dated May 18–June 2 [1906], and pp. 7–198 containing various accounts, some of which do not appear to be in Porter's handwriting; six letters from Cook to Porter; a copy of Champ's letter, 1906, recommending Porter to Walter H. Brooks; and thirteen letters, 1907, between Cook and Porter concerning money that Cook owed Porter.

[5] Porter's Diary, 1906, p. 1, has a brief narrative of the Indian ponies, or cayuses, bought on the Yakima Reservation for this trip.

[6] For Porter's description of the voyage to Sitka and beyond, see ibid., pp. 2–3.

behind. Three of us—the doctor, Browne, and myself—first made a reconnaissance that resulted in as strenuous work as I had ever been put through. With packs on our backs, we hiked up a valley with a glacial stream. As the stream meandered from wall to wall, there was almost continuous wading in the ice water. Several times we lost our footing. But there was always wood about, stranded on the bars, and the warmth from a big fire will let one forget a lot of past torture. A somewhat hasty judgment convinced us that the pass was negotiable. So we returned to bring up the main party.

Our judgment proved faulty. The pass ended in box canyons that no horses could get through. The northern slopes of the range were barred here, and there was nothing left but to return and work along the southern slopes until abreast of the big mountain.

Whatever faults Dr. Cook may be accused of, the trip up that glacial stream brought out his sterling qualities as a companion in such pioneer work. Always in good spirits and ready for more than his share of the drudgery, resourceful, and considerate of the others.

Somewhere along the trail, an Indian, Pete by name, had attached himself to the party to show us the trails. It was perhaps well that he did, for at times there were no trails.

At last, McKinley stood out in full view, fifteen miles away, to be sure, but towering over us by 19,000 feet. (Our elevation here, at the foot of the Tokichitna [Tokositna] Glacier, was about a thousand feet above sea level).[7] All snow and ice from 3,000 feet up. That is the unique thing about Mount McKinley as a climbing proposition. Most other high peaks are nearer the equator, and base camps can be established at snow line with pack animals some 15,000 feet up. Not so here. Ice conditions begin almost at sea level.

The southern slopes were carefully scanned through telescopes to find a possible route. Avalanches everywhere. Possibly the northeast slope could be negotiated.

"Here's what we will do," said the doctor. "There's no possibility of making the

[7] The official elevation of Mount McKinley is 20,320 feet at the south peak and 19,470 feet at the north peak (Donald J. Orth, "Dictionary of Alaska Place Names," *U.S. Geological Survey, Professional Paper*, No. 567 [Washington, D.C., 1967], 1 and 610).

ascent from this side. We will disband, to meet together at tidewater in September. You, Browne, go over into the Yentna region to collect zoological specimens. Porter, you take your time going back and clear up the map among the peaks west of McKinley, and I'll take the *Bolshoy* and go up the Susitna and have a look at the northeast slope. We will go back to the States and come out again next year."

No sooner said than done. I was several weeks clearing up three thousand miles of hitherto unknown peaks and glaciers.[8] Coming finally to the river that would bring us down to the rendezvous, we (I had two men with me) built a raft and upon it stowed the instruments and camp gear. There remained the hard task of disposing of our two faithful pack animals. The other men would not do it. So the hateful job was left for me. Shooting was the most merciful thing to do. Certainly, if left to themselves, the coming winter would bring an end far more terrible.

In three days we were at Susitna Station. Scarcely had we arrived before a commotion down by the shore brought us to the river's bank.

There was the *Bolshoy*, with Dr. Cook at the stern and Barrill the packer just stepping ashore.

"Go back and congratulate the doctor," he said as I reached the boat.

"How so?"

"He got to the top."

Well, so it seemed. They described a hair-raising dash to the very summit. Following the Tokichitna Glacier they had climbed the northeast spur, digging into the very face of vertical ice walls when night overtook them. The account was all very thrilling, and at that time I believe it was accepted as truth by everyone in the party.

I returned east with the doctor and helped to illustrate (from verbal descriptions)

[8] Porter prepared a "Reconnaissance map of region south of Mt. McKinley, Alaska, including the Yentna Mining District. F. A. Cook in charge. Triangulation and topography by R. W. Porter. Surveyed in 1906. Scale 1:250,000 . . . contour interval, 200 feet." This map was published by the U.S. Geological Survey and its information incorporated into a "Reconnaissance Map of Mt. McKinley Region, Alaska, Edition 1907." For information about this survey, see Porter, "Surveys by Cook party in 1906," in *The Mount McKinley Region, Alaska*, by Alfred H. Brooks, published in *U.S. Geological Survey, Professional Paper*, No. 70 (Washington, D.C., 1911), 39–42.

*Mount McKinley looking north, as seen from the ridge between
the Tokichitna and Tococha glaciers.*

the book he was preparing. (Sometime during the Cook-Peary controversy, I ran across a statement in the paper that Barrill had denied having reached the summit, that the events pictured in Cook's volume *To the Top of the Continent* never happened, that they were figments of the doctor's imagination.)[9] I worked up the field notes of the trip, which were afterwards incorporated in the maps of the Geological Survey.[10]

But evidently doubts began to assail some of the party, for soon Browne and Parker were back in Alaska following up the doctor's trail over the Tokichitna Glacier.[11] They later published a photograph of a mountain summit said to be several miles from McKinley's peak and but five or six thousand feet elevation, which to all appearances is identical with the peak shown in the doctor's book and labeled "The Top of the Continent." I have the two photographs before me now, and the one by Browne and Parker certainly looks like damaging evidence. For, while the snowbanks are unlike, as might be expected with an interval of some year's time, the topographical features are alike in every detail.

[9] *To the Top of the Continent: Discovery, Exploration, and Adventure in Sub-Arctic Alaska, the First Ascent of Mt. McKinley* (New York, 1908). The frontispiece of this book is a color-plate reproduction of Porter's beautiful watercolor entitled "Mt. McKinley, 20,390 feet, Highest Mountain in North America" with the note "from a painting by Russell W. Porter." This watercolor is with the Porter Papers. The only other reference to Porter in Cook's book is in the title of the miner's map of the Mount McKinley region, between pp. 152 and 153, which states simply "by the Topographer of the Cook–Mt. McKinley Expedition, 1907." Problems arose between Cook and Porter when Porter requested payment for the map and various illustrations. This correspondence is also with the Porter Papers.

[10] A search of the records of the U.S. Geological Survey, Record Group 57, in the National Archives has failed to disclose the existence of Porter's field notes and planetable work. In 1909 Peary corresponded with the U.S. Geological Survey and with Porter concerning these field notes and Porter's topographic map of the Mount McKinley region. Porter obtained a published copy of the map and annotated it with various lines to indicate routes that he, Cook, and others traveled. This map and the correspondence are among the Peary Papers, RG 401 (1A).

[11] See Belmore Browne and Herschel C. Parker, *The Conquest of Mount McKinley: The Story of Three Expeditions through the Alaskan Wilderness to Mount McKinley, North America's Highest and Most Inaccessible Mountain* (New York, 1913).

Chapter 11

WELL, HERE WE ARE at the end of the trail, the trail that I hit such a "resounding whack" with the exuberance of youth forty years ago. What of the findings? Are there any lessons to be wrung from this long chase after the arctic goddess. Just for fun, I took a string and on a globe measured off the trail windings over the earth's surface covering the ten expeditions.[1] It came out well over a hundred thousand miles, almost half way to the moon. For distance traveled, this might well be a record.

Hadn't that elusive siren left me anything as compensation for all this toil, something to chalk up on the balance sheet not in the red? Ah, yes. Strange as it may seem, and perhaps unwittingly, she had played into my hands. For I am now living a normal life again with my fellowmen and earning my daily bread at a calling directly traceable to the bitter cold nights in latitude 82, happy in my work as probably few men are happy. Thank you, my fair goddess, you taught me how to labor and make of it a labor of love.

Back in chapter nine was described the little observatory perched on a pile of rocks within eight degrees of the pole where night after night I communed with the stars through an instrument called a vertical transit.[2] As time passed on and the observations accumulated, I began to realize the significance of just what was happening. Here was I, with this wizard of a thing barely a foot square, locating

---

[1] Porter participated in the following expeditions:

    Cook's arctic expedition in the *Miranda*, 1894

    Peary's two arctic expeditions in the *Hope*, 1896 and 1897

    Porter's expedition to British Columbia, 1898

    Porter's expedition to Labrador, etc., 1899

    Peary Arctic Club Relief expedition in the *Diana*, 1899

    Baldwin-Ziegler arctic expedition to Franz Josef Land, 1901–2

    Fiala-Ziegler arctic expedition to Franz Josef Land, 1903–5

    Cook's Mount McKinley expedition, 1906

    Porter-Bryant expedition to Eastern Labrador, 1912.

[2] See chap. 8, pp. 102–12.

myself on the earth's surface to within a few feet of the actual truth, finding the time of day to a fraction of a second. Through its intricate mechanism I was drawn farther afield, out into the great spaces where our little family of planets was traveling. Such law and order! It was a marvel.

I think this understanding of how the celestial mechanism behaves, how every motion of the sun, moon, and stars can be explained and brought into accord with hard-and-fast mathematics, was the cause that whetted my curiosity to know more about these instruments of precision: What were they made of? How could they do this and that? What principle of design governed their design? What powerful tool was responsible for all this exactitude? At last the secret came out—light!

Light. Now to me the most wonderful of all natural phenomena. Commonplace as the air we breathe. Mysterious in its workings as the constitution of the atom. Its inconceivable velocity. What a shock to know that an object is not always where you see it. Take the sun up there. It is not where it looks to be at all. The light that forms its image on your retina left the sun eight minutes before it reached your eye. Meanwhile, she had moved on.

As the properties of light became more familiar, so did the means by which it could be picked to pieces, bent, split up into its different parts. Lenses, prisms, mirrors, gratings—all took on a new significance. Here surely was something worth tying to, something to go into further later on.

The opportunity came on the return from the Mount McKinley trip. Sick with the failures of ten years' effort, I pulled up stakes, cut loose from the cities, and with my household goods acquired a beautiful spot of fifty acres on the Maine coast, well away from summer crowds.[3] Here I could work undisturbed. The white goddess had at last ceased calling.

I was not long finding out that the optical hobby was an expensive one to ride. I wanted a telescope, and a big one. To buy it would cost over a thousand dollars. Was

[3] Here Porter is referring to a small peninsula that extends south along the west side of the entrance to Penobscot Bay about sixty-five miles from Portland, Me. The nearest settlement is Port Clyde, referred to by Porter as Land's End, in Saint George Township, which in 1970 had a permanent population of 400.

From a photograph - These walruses paid little attention
to us - The fellow nearest the dog must have been very old   Among my color notes
I fend the following " The bull (lying down) probably very old. Hide resembled that of enormous
toad (Stretch out your fingers straight and note the wrinkles over the middle joints) He reminds
me when moving of the working of the bones and joints of an elephant when walking."

The walruses paid little attention to us.

there no other way? Couldn't I make it? Of all things, to make a powerful telescope with one's own hands. Preposterous! And yet I had the nerve to try.

Down in the cellar of the old farmhouse a barrel was installed, fastened to the stone-flagged floor. On the barrelhead was secured a round disk of glass two inches thick. Upon this disk I slowly moved another, back and forth, round and round, back and forth. I could hear the emery cutting away the glass to the proper curve. The lens—or mirror, rather—was gradually forming. Later, with a red powder the polish began to appear. Hooray!

The summer was gone before the lens was finished. But in a telescope, the lens (mirror) is the whole thing. The tube is only incidental as a means of holding the eyepiece rigidly at a fixed distance from the lens. The rest was easy, but those long hours around the barrel opened my eyes to the wonders of an optical surface. Even the thought that I was measuring errors of only a millionth of an inch had a kick to it. And the means by which these delicate tests were made—an oil lamp and a kitchen knife! Why, anybody with a little common sense and patience and a knack of using his two hands could do the same thing. Well, why didn't they? So far as I could see, it was only the lack of a few available instructions as to how to go at it. Here at last was a real job, to show the way to others.

It was fortunate that the publicity tool was already at hand, that such an old established magazine as the *Scientific American* lent a willing ear. Soon a series of articles on the subject of amateur telescope making, then a book that has now gone into its third edition.[4] It seems almost incredible, but thousands of fellows have

[4] "Mirror Making and Mounting a Sun Telescope, Literature and Materials," *Amateur Telescope Making*, ed. Albert G. Ingalls (New York, 1926).

The following other publications by Porter from 1916 through 1929 also indicate his great interest in popularizing astronomy and in making telescopes and related instruments: "Astronomy in the Arctic: Some of the Duties and Hardships in the Frigid North," *Scientific American*, Supplement, 79 (1915), 39; "Amateur's Observatory," ibid., 84 (1917), 68–69; "The Enclosed Observatory Room," ibid., 85 (1918), 277; "A New Form of Mounting for Large Reflectors," ibid., 86 (1918), 77; "Mirror Making for Reflecting Telescopes," ibid., 134 (1926), 86–89; "Literature and Materials for Telescope Mirror Making," ibid., p. 117; "Mountings for Reflecting Telescopes," ibid., pp. 164–67; "Simple Study in Optics," ibid., 137 (1927), 421; "The Polar Reflecting Telescope: An Amateur's Attempt at an Observatory That May Be Made Comfortable in Cold Weather," *Popular Astronomy*, 24

done the trick and thoroughly enjoyed it. Clubs of enthusiasts have sprung up in the cities. And there the ground had lain, fallow, ready for anyone to come and plow the furrow. Strange that indirectly I could thank the goddess for all this.

Then came the World War. A very dear friend of mine, Governor Hartness of Vermont (then food administrator) wrote me.[5] "The war has cut off our supply of optical glass. We are doing our utmost to make it ourselves. You are needed at the Bureau of Standards in Washington. Pack your bag and get down there as soon as you can."[6]

Followed a year (until the Armistice), helping where I could to speed the production of the optical parts that go into range finders, binoculars, sextants, etc. From there, the trail led back to my old home in Vermont. Down in the governor's dugout under his lawn we went into executive session.

"Here's a job well worthy of your attention," he said. "You know all about a screw, of course—common unobtrusive things, hard to find an object anywhere that hasn't got a screw in it somewhere holding it together. In principle, only a wedge wound around a cylinder. But the screw is one of the worst offenders in the mechanical world, forever coming loose, shearing off—often a menace to safety. Rivets are far more trustworthy as fasteners, but unfortunately they cannot always be used. We must have screws, better screws, for a screw that's well made and fits perfectly in its mating part is a good thing."

(1916), 308–17; "The Theodolite for Testing Telescopic Specula: A New Use for a Familiar Instrument," ibid., pp. 370–71; "The Enclosed Observatory Room," ibid., 25 (1917), 296–300; "A New Form of Mounting for Large Reflectors," ibid., 26 (1918), 147–49; "Latitude without Instruments," ibid., 29 (1921), 197–204; "A New Mounting for a Reflecting Telescope," ibid., pp. 249–51; "The Telescope Makers of Springfield, Vermont," ibid., 31 (1923), 153–62; and "Stellafane," ibid., 35 (1927), 501–5. For a narrative on Porter's contributions to astronomy, see James Stokley, "He Showed Thousands the Stars," *Science Newsletter*, 16 (1929), 349–51.

[5] James Hartness. For his biography, see *National Cyclopaedia of American Biography*, 30 (1918), 34. With the Porter Papers, RG 401 (27–B), is correspondence, most of it from 1913 through 1918, from Hartness, president of the Jones & Lamson Machine Company of Springfield, Vt.

[6] Porter's employment with the National Bureau of Standards during World War I, 1917–1918, is documented in the records of that government agency (Record Group 167) in the National Archives.

All this was easy to follow, but I couldn't see just where I came into the picture. I knew nothing about screws.

"Oh, you'll see all right when I explain. I've hit on a way of projecting a screw on a screen a hundred times its actual size in such a way that it shows up all the errors, separates the sheep from the goats, the shirkers from the trusties. It's an optical machine. Now go to it. Perfect the instrument so we can put it on the market."[7]

The idea, simple as it was, showed the divine spark of the inventor. It took years to knock the thing into shape so that it was foolproof. Strange to say, it found a wider field in things other than screws. In hundreds of factories today it is passing judgment on such things as phonograph needles, light filaments, dental burrs, spark plugs, hair clippers—all sorts of peculiar shapes that are difficult or impossible to inspect mechanically.[8] And then came the big surprise that filled my cup of happiness to the brim.

There had been rumors in the papers and magazines from time to time of a proposed telescope that was to be several times as large as any yet built, a colossal undertaking for which funds had already been secured.[9] What a privilege to be able to have a hand in such a venture. Was it a coincidence that, years before, I had designed a mounting for a supertelescope such as this?

The governor called me into his dugout. With him were two astronomers from Pasadena. Could what I heard them saying be true, that I was wanted out there to help in the effort?[10]

And so these last lines are being penned under sunny skies. I often recall that

[7] James Hartness developed his proposal to Porter in a letter, dated Oct. 18, 1918, which is among the Porter Papers.

[8] Porter's invention is described in *The Hartness Screw Thread Comparator for Accurate and Rapid Screw Gaging* (Springfield, Vt.: Jones & Lamson Machine Company, 1921), with drawings and sketches by Porter. There is no reference, however, to Porter's contributions, including drawings and sketches. A specimen model of this machine is on display at the National Museum of History and Technology, the Smithsonian Institution, Washington, D.C. (1975).

[9] This was the proposed 200-inch telescope for Mount Palomar.

[10] Porter was on the staff primarily responsible for the design, construction, and assembly of the 200-inch telescope for Mount Palomar. Most of the work was accomplished at the California

pledge made when Butland and I were dragging our sleeping bags through the snow—frozen feet and fingers—fighting for our very lives: "If I ever get out of this, I'm going to the Equator and stay there." And his reply: "Me for New York." Well, I am not on the Equator but considerably nearer to it than the Pole, in fact nearer to it than the rigors of a New England winter. I have no ax to grind with my northern sweetheart now. All things come to those who wait.

Institute of Technology in Pasadena. There are relatively few notes concerning this work among the Porter Papers. The archives of the California Institute of Technology in Pasadena, the Mount Palomar Observatory, and possibly the Mount Wilson Observatory, north of Pasadena, however, have considerable information on Porter's role in the successful completion and use of the world-famous telescope. See the following publications for additional information on Porter's contributions in the telescope's development: Fassero and Porter, *Photographic Giants of Palomar*, with drawings by Porter; Albert G. Ingalls, "Operation of the Grinding Machine for the 200-inch Pyrex Telescope Disk in Pasadena," *Scientific American*, 155 (1936), 100; Porter and James A. Anderson, "The 200-inch Telescope," *The Telescope*, 7 (1940), 29–39; David Oakes Woodbury, *The Glass Giant of Palomar, with 50 Drawings by the Author and Sketches by Russell W. Porter* (New York, 1939); and Porter, "Silvering the World's Largest Telescope: A Witness Describes This Fascinating Process," *Scientific American*, 141 (1929), 225.

Russell Williams Porter: Selected Bibliography

Obituaries

"Death of Russell W. Porter." *Astronomical Society of the Pacific, Publications*, 61 (April 1949), 110.

"Russell W. Porter." *New York Times*, Feb. 29, 1949.

"Russell W. Porter." *Science*, 109 (Mar. 4, 1949), 243.

"Russell W. Porter." *Time Magazine*, Mar. 7, 1949, p. 87.

Works about Porter

Ingalls, Albert G. "The Heavens Declare the Glory of God: How a Group of Enthusiasts Learned to Make Telescopes and Became Amateur Astronomers." *Scientific American*, 133 (1925), 293–95.

———. "Telescopics." *Scientific American*, 174 (1945), 285.

———. "How the Patron Saint of the Amateur Telescope-building Hobby First Took Up Telescope Making." *Scientific American*, 165 (1941), 235.

———. "The Amateur Astronomer." *Scientific American*, 180 (1949), 60–63.

Marshall, Oscar S. "Russell W. Porter, 1871–1949." *Popular Astronomy*, 57 (1949), 235–40.

Milan, Dennis. "A Russell W. Porter Exhibit." *Sky & Telescope*, 34 (1967), 226–28.

Pendray, G. Edward. "Amateur Telescope-makers and How They Have Advanced the Art." *Men, Mirrors, and Stars.* New York, 1939, pp. 270–78.

"Porter, Russell Williams." *Dictionary of American Biography*, Supplement Four. New York, 1974.

Scanlon, Les and Margaret. "R.W.P.—Telescope Artist." *Sky & Telescope*, 8 (1949), 143–45.

Waldron, W. "One Really Happy Man." *American Magazine*, November 1931, pp. 50–51.

Willard, Berton C. "Russell W. Porter . . . Explorer." *Polar Notes.* Dartmouth College Library, No. 8 (1968), 69–84.

———. *Russell W. Porter: Arctic Explorer, Artist, and Telescope Maker.* Freeport, Me., forthcoming.

Woodbury, David O. "The Men." *The Glass Giant of Palomar.* Illustrated with Drawings by the Author and Sketches by Russell W. Porter, and Photos. New York, 1953, pp. 109–13.

Porter's Publications on Arctic Subjects

"Artist in Greenland." *New England Magazine*, NS, 16 (1897), 289–303.

"Frobisher Bay Revisited." *American Geographical Society Journal (Bulletin)*, 30 (1898), 97–110.

"Hudson Bay Trading Post." *New England Magazine*, NS, 20 (1899), 715–21.

"Astronomical Observations and Reductions." In *The Ziegler Polar Expedition, 1903–1905 . . . Scientific Results Obtained under the Direction of William J. Peters.* Washington, D.C., 1907, pp. 597–622.

"Map Construction and Survey Work." In *The Ziegler Polar Expedition, 1903–1905 . . . Scientific Results Obtained under the Direction of William J. Peters.* Washington, D.C., 1907, pp. 623–30.

"Surveys by Cook Party in 1906." In Alfred H. Brooks, "The Mount McKinley Region, Alaska. . . ." *U.S. Geological Survey, Professional Paper*, No. 70. Washington, D.C., 1911, pp. 39–42.

Tooloogah